The First Christian

Karen Armstrong  ...ught up in the
country and in Bir... glish teaching
order of nuns and ...bedience in 1965.
In 1967 the order sent her to Oxford University to read English language
and literature with a view to teaching in one of their schools. She left the
order in 1969 but continued at Oxford, where she graduated in 1970 and
began to study for a research degree. During her seven years as a nun, she
studied theology and Church history, and eventually worked towards a
diploma in theology.

From 1973 to 1976 she held the post of tutorial research fellow at Bedford
College and taught nineteenth- and twentieth-century literature at
London University. She later taught English in a girls' school for six years
and is now a freelance writer living in London.

Karen Armstrong is the author of two autobiographical works, *Through
the Narrow Gate* and *Beginning the World*.

Karen Armstrong

The First Christian

Saint Paul's impact on Christianity

Pan Original
Pan Books London and Sydney

For Abed and Anat Zubi
and their sons, Adam and Amir,
for their warmth and generous
friendship and for sharing with me
their last glimpses of Israel
before they had to leave it.

First published 1983 by Pan Books Ltd,
Cavaye Place, London SW10 9PG
© Karen Armstrong 1983
Maps by Ken Smith
Picture research by Philippa Lewis
ISBN 0 330 28161 5
Photoset by Parker Typesetting Service, Leicester
Printed in Great Britain by
Cox & Wyman Ltd, Reading

Contents

Illustrations

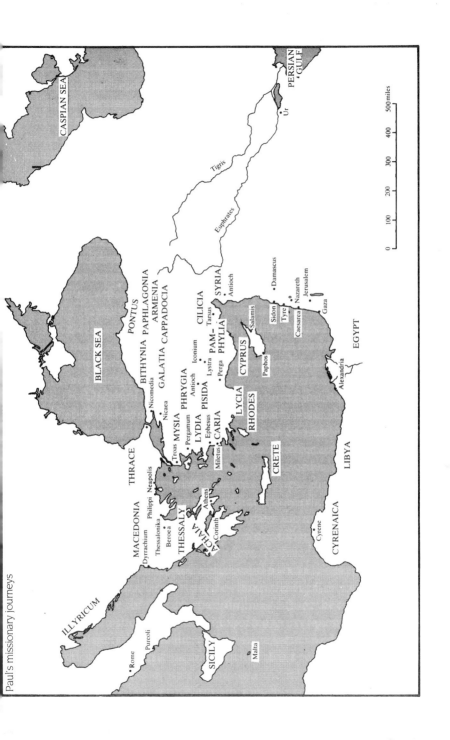

Paul's missionary journeys

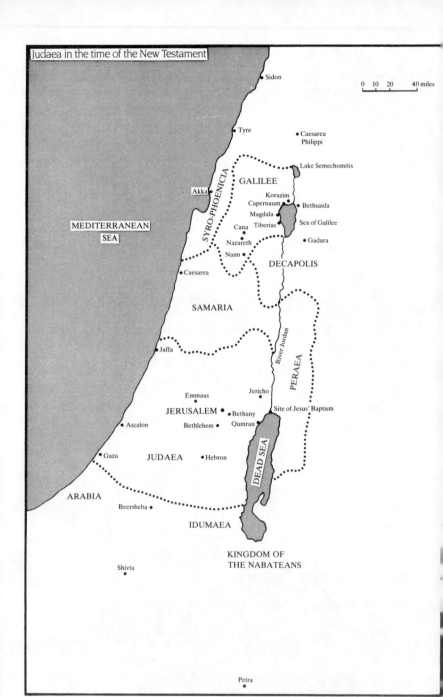

Judaea in the time of the New Testament

0   10   20   40 miles

Sidon

Tyre

Caesarea
Philippi

Lake Semechomitis

GALILEE

Akka

Korazim

Capernaum
Magdala
Cana
Tiberias

Bethsaida

Sea of Galilee

Nazareth

Gadara

Naim

DECAPOLIS

MEDITERRANEAN
SEA

Caesarea

SAMARIA

SYRO-PHOENICIA

Jaffa

River Jordan

PERAEA

Emmaus

Jericho

JERUSALEM

Bethany

Site of Jesus' Baptism

Ascalon

Bethlehem

Qumran

Gaza

JUDAEA

Hebron

DEAD SEA

ARABIA

Beersheba

IDUMAEA

KINGDOM OF
THE NABATEANS

Shivta

Petra

Acknowledgements

There are many people who have helped me with my study of St Paul. First of all I must thank Dr Michael Goulder of the University of Birmingham, who was appointed adviser to the television series by Channel 4. He not only helped me with his fine New Testament scholarship and his painstaking and sympathetic reading of the television scripts as I was writing them, but also with his good-humoured patience with my mistakes and kind encouragement. On some points we disagree, but he most generously shared with me his knowledge and corrected my inaccuracies, and he will find many of his admirable suggestions in these pages. I thank him for filling out my knowledge of first-century Christianity with the fruits of his life-long study.

Equal thanks must go to Amnon Teitelbaum, the director of the television series for Kastel Communications Ltd. He showed me his country, Israel, in the most inspiring way while I was there researching for the series and I am most grateful to him for his knowledge of the history and archaeology of Israel. While I was writing the scripts, he came over to England and was of invaluable help in his quick insights about how I could fit my ideas to the visual material available. Above all, I thank him for his friendship throughout the project, for his tact and sensitivity during the series and his excellent ideas and generous encouragement.

I must also thank everybody at Kastel Communications for their warm welcome and kindness to me during my time in Jerusalem. Particularly I should like to thank Micah Shagrir, the president of Kastel, and Daniel Dadia, Amnon's assistant, who drove me round the whole of Israel twice and gave me a taste for fast Israeli driving, as well as being unfailingly helpful and cheerful during the inevitable crises. Special thanks must also go to the Kastel film crew, who made the filming so enjoyable. They accepted me as one of themselves and were always encouraging, friendly and kind, patient when I made a mistake, and good humoured when anything went wrong. They taught me how to be an Israeli.

I am particularly grateful also to Hyam Maccoby, who during our talks together helped me towards a fuller under-standing of Judaism with his scholarship, intuition and imaginative insight. He was most generous with his time, encouragement and help.

John Ranelagh of Channel 4 Television, who commissioned me to write the series, I must thank very specially for his faith in me and his support throughout what has probably been the most enjoyable work of my life. He also read the scripts and made some very helpful and important suggestions. I am also very grateful to Nicholas Fraser and Adam Clapham, of Griffin Productions, who gave me some valuable hints about filming and television presentation.

Finally, nothing would have been written at all had it not been for my two very good friends Rosanne Musgrave and Caroline Kirby. While I was writing the scripts and the first draft of this book I was temporarily homeless. Following the gospel precept as well as their instincts of unfailing generosity, they both at times took me in and provided a roof over my head, beautifully cooked meals, drinks at critical moments, typewriters and an indispensable moral support. I thank them both most sincerely.

Introduction

St Paul has always been a hero of mine. I admire the courage of a man who almost single-handed laid the foundations of the Church in Syria, Asia Minor and Europe and who covered thousands of miles on foot or using only the most basic means of travel through inhospitable country. Nor was it simply a question of guts. Paul was a brilliant man; he created Christian theology, and sometimes it seems as though he was even more important to Christianity than Jesus Christ. There is also something very refreshing about Paul. I like his passion and his enthusiasm. I like his vulnerability, his occasional personal diffidence. After reading the lives of many Christian saints, it is a relief to read about one who can get angry instead of piously and inevitably turning the other cheek and who is not too superior in virtue to want to be loved by his converts.

Yet my admiration is tinged with uneasiness, an uneasiness that has developed alongside my worries about Christianity. There is in Christianity a morbidity. There is a masochism that exalts pain and suffering, an unhealthy rejection of the body and sensuous pleasure. There is an intolerance which has often expressed itself in violent persecutions and crusades against Jews, infidels and, appallingly, within the Christian ranks against 'heretics' or people whose opinions of dogma differ from those of the governing authority. There is a complacency and a smugness which often refuses challenge of any sort, and there is also a strange alliance with secular power and worldly riches. I say 'strange' because of the life of Jesus of Nazareth, who urged his followers to leave their possessions and follow him into poverty. It has sometimes seemed to me that Christ would find it difficult to recognise certain elements in Christianity if he returned to earth today. Of course I have been able to see that the worrying side of Christianity does not constitute its whole, that there are many worthy Christians who are equally concerned about these matters and whose lives are an imitation of the Christ of the gospels. Christianity has inspired Elizabeth Fry and Mother Theresa to lives of charity at its best, for example. However, my worries have persisted as I have read more and more Church history and looked around contemporary Christianity. The unhealthy aspects of Christianity are there and I can see that they could all find an origin in the Epistles of St Paul.

As I read the Epistles, my admiration persists for the inspiring and beautifully written account Paul gives of the Christian life. But frequently too I wince. As a woman, I do not like Paul for saying that a woman should keep a seemly silence at meetings because she is inferior to man. I worry about Paul's dislike of the body and his denigration of sexual love. I can see in his proud boasting about his sufferings the beginnings of Christian masochism and the search for suffering for suffering's sake. Sometimes he writes movingly about the Jews; at other times he seems anti-semitic. In his fierce insistence on the supremacy of his own gospel I can see the beginnings of Christian authoritarianism and intolerance. It appears wrong that he supports institutions like slavery and shows no interest in social change. On the contrary, his admiration for the Roman Empire and the governing authorities seems to mark the beginning of that involvement with the secular arm which has distracted Christianity away from her true spiritual interests.

Even when I turn back to study the life and teachings of

Jesus it seems that Paul has not only been an important influence on Christianity, but that in a very real sense he was its founder. He could be called the first Christian.

When I was invited to write the scripts for a television series on St Paul and this book, I was delighted. It seemed an admirable way of coming to grips with the paradox that Paul presented for me. Now with the opportunity I had to concentrate on the Epistles one of my worries evaporated. It is true that many of the unpleasant aspects of Christianity find their origin in Paul, but he had no idea of the extent of his responsibility. When he was writing his letters he never considered that for two thousand years Christians would be poring over his words and building their own sometimes dubious theologies on top of them. This was not due simply to humility – rather it was because he was convinced that the world as we know it would have passed away. Paul was expecting Christ's glorious return within his own lifetime, and was legislating for a few years only. The paradoxes that he imposed on his converts were the paradoxes endemic to a time of crisis: Paul believed he was living in the 'last days' of the world. Two thousand years later the paradoxes have hardened into the Christianity we have today.

Note: Biblical quotations have been taken from *The Jerusalem Bible*.

1 Paul of Tarsus and Jesus of Nazareth

It is often said, by Christians as well as by those who reject the Christian message, that the worst thing that ever happened to Christianity was St Paul. It is said that he perverted the simple, loving message of Jesus and transformed it into something complicated, theological, even unhealthy. Paul, says Nietzsche, nailed Jesus to the cross by his theology: 'His life, example, teaching and death as well as the meaning and right of the whole gospel. Nothing remained when this counterfeiter conceived in hatred that of which he alone could make use.' Yet when we examine the gospel stories and the early history of Christianity, Paul, instead of distorting the Christian message, can be seen as its great originator. Time and again in the history of Christianity, whenever there has been a reforming movement, its inspiration has been not Jesus so much as Paul. Augustine, Luther, Calvin, Barth, even the second Vatican council, all claim Paul as their mentor and inspiration.

Paul and Jesus were contemporaries, although they never met. Their backgrounds were quite different, but one thing they did have in common: both were Jews, members of God's 'chosen people'. For both men their race and religion were of crucial significance. For both men Jerusalem was the centre of the world; the Holy Land of Israel was sacred as the gift of God to his people. Both men were proud to be Jews until the day they died.

Yet although their Judaism was a most important link

between Paul and Jesus, there was an important difference. Jesus spent all his life in the Holy Land. As a Jew of Judaea he had different preoccupations from Paul, who was a Jew of the diaspora. Paul belonged to one of those scattered communities of Jews that by the first century were to be found throughout the Roman Empire. It used to be thought that the diaspora Jews differed greatly from their Judaean brethren and that they were far more affected by the Hellenistic world that surrounded them. But nowadays we try not to exaggerate the difference. The most famous contemporaneous Jew of the diaspora was Philo of Alexandria, who attempted to reinterpret the Old Testament in the light of the philosophy of Plato. But Philo, though widely known, was by no means typical. Most diaspora Jews clung as closely as they could to Judaean practice and resisted the lures of Hellenism. The author of the Gospel According to St Matthew was, before his conversion to Christianity, a Jew of the diaspora, and his gospel presents a very conservative approach to Judaism.

Paul was born in Tarsus in Cilicia, modern Turkey. We know practically nothing about his early life, but what we can deduce shows that, despite his Jewish link with Jesus, the circumstances of his upbringing and education were very different. Tarsus was one of the Greek cities in the empire which the Romans allowed to be self-governing. Here Antony had met Cleopatra when she sailed up the river Cydnus in her gilt barge. Tarsus was a key trading centre, and merchants came from both the Mediterranean and from Galatea and Cappadocia, giving the city a bustling, cosmopolitan atmosphere. Tarsus was also a university town, an important centre of the Stoic philosophy. It was a thriving and sophisticated Greek city.

Paul spoke and wrote in Greek. He knew Hebrew, as any devout Jew would, but he seems to have read the Old Testament in its Greek translation, the Septuagint. In Acts of the Apostles the author claims that Paul studied the

Torah (the Law of Moses) in Jerusalem, under the famous Pharisee, Rabbi Gamaliel. In his letters Paul never mentions Gamaliel, and some scholars have doubted Acts on this point. Certainly, before his conversion Paul was a Pharisee, and as there were no Pharisees in Tarsus – Pharisaism was a purely Judaean movement – he must have travelled from Cilicia to Judaea at some time. Thus, although he was Greek speaking, Paul was perhaps not much touched by the culture of the Greek world, but rather extended his intellectual energies on Judaic studies. He seems to have known no Greek literature and practically no Greek philosophy. A few popular Stoic ideas creep into the Epistles from time to time, but Paul's use of them is superficial and they are not organic to his thought. The mainspring of his life before his conversion to Jesus seems to have been his Judaism. He never mentions Tarsus in his letters, but he does write proudly about his race and religion:

> I was born of the race of Israel and of the tribe of Benjamin, a Hebrew born of Hebrew parents, and I was circumcised when I was eight days old. As for the Law, I was a Pharisee; as for working for religion, I was a persecutor of the Church; as far as the Law can make you perfect I was faultless.

(Philippians 3: 5-6)

Although many aspects of the Greco-Roman world passed him by, there was one circumstance of Paul's birth in Tarsus which deeply affected his life and which would leave an indelible mark on Christianity. Paul was a Roman citizen. How he had come by this privilege we have no idea. It may have been that his family once gave some service to the empire which was rewarded by citizenship. Paul was all his life a proud supporter of the Roman Empire. As a Roman citizen living in a free Greek city, he had a very different upbringing from Jesus, who was living in a country that had been defeated and occupied by the Romans and whose inhabitants were far from being lovers and admirers of the empire. Before we can fully understand Paul we have to spend some time considering the life and times of Jesus, on whom Paul based completely his own life.

For the Jews of Judaea, the Roman occupation was not just a political matter. It was also a religious issue. When God called Abraham out of Ur of the Chaldees, he entered into a covenant or solemn agreement with him. Abraham was to be the founder of a new race, specially dedicated to God. When, following God's directions, Abraham arrived in the land of Canaan, modern Israel and Palestine, God promised to give him the land:

> Yahweh said to Abraham after Lot had parted company with him, 'Look all round from where you are towards the north and the south, towards the east and the west. All the land within sight I will give to you and your descendants for ever. I will make your descendants like the dust on the ground: when men succeed in counting the specks of dust on the ground, then they will be able to count your descendants! Come, travel through the length and breadth of the land, for I mean to give it to you.'
>
> (Genesis 13: 14-17)

From the moment of their birth as the 'chosen race', the land belonged to the Jews. The Romans, therefore, were usurpers and were in a sense usurping God. When Solomon built his Temple in Jerusalem, God dwelt there with his people, ruling the land. In the holy of holies, his 'presence' (the *shekinah*) dwelt in the heart of the holy city. Occupation, therefore, was a religious outrage. Since the return from the exile in Babylon, the Jews had lost their political independence and for some five hundred years they had been subject to a long succession of foreign powers: the Persians, the Macedonians, the Egyptians, the Seleucids, the Parthians and finally the Romans. Yet still, five centuries later, they were not able to reconcile themselves to the notion of subjection, so deeply did it contradict their religion.

The Roman occupation was an unpleasant one. At first, when the Romans conquered the province of Judaea, as it became known, they installed a vassal king, the Idumaean Jew, Herod. Herod was a brilliant man with a reputation for cruelty. He was a thorough-going Hellenist, deeply distrusted by his subjects because of his Greek way of life. He immediately started a huge building project in the Holy Land, the most significant work being the rebuilding of the Temple, which was completed – or at least was being used – by the time of Jesus' birth in about 7 BC. Herod's beautiful buildings, however, did nothing to endear him to his subjects, who rejoiced heartily when he died in 4 BC. Their happiness was short-lived. His kingdom was divided between his three sons; Philip took the north-east part of the kingdom, Herod Antipas ruled Galilee and part of the land to the east of the Jordan, and was thus the sovereign of Jesus and of John the Baptist, and Archelaus took Samaria and Judaea with Jerusalem.

All these remained puppet states of short duration. The first to go was Judaea after the brutal Archelaus was deposed. The territory was annexed in AD 6 to the Roman province of Syria, and was governed by a Roman procurator, with police power to control public order and the power to execute political opponents of Roman rule. To have a Roman governing the Holy Land was felt as a deep national disgrace, even though the Romans allowed the Jews complete religious freedom. Herod, unpopular because he was a foreigner, had at least been a Jew. To have the Roman governor in his residence at Caesarea and to have the Roman Fortress Antonia directly overlooking the Temple were reminders of the foreign usurpation. In addition, the troops were third rate and the governor extorted gross taxes to line his own pockets. The smallest opposition to the regime was punished with crucifixion, a death the Jews abhorred on religious grounds.

It is not clear how much revolutionary activity against

Rome there was during Jesus' lifetime, although it was once thought that there was a good deal. Tacitus tells us that under Emperor Tiberias there was peace throughout the empire: 'Sub Tiberio quies.' However, mainstream Judaism was deeply concerned about the political situation.

There were two principal parties in Judaic Judaism at that time: the Pharisees and the Sadducees. Both were involved in politics. The Sadducees – consisting of the aristocracy and the rich priestly families – cooperated with the Romans. They believed that opposition to Rome was futile and that rebellion could lead only to disaster. They were proved right: in AD 66 the great Jewish revolt broke out in Caesarea and, after holding Rome at bay for an astonishing four years, the Jewish rebels were defeated in AD 70. Jerusalem was devastated, the Temple destroyed; thousands of Jews lost their lives and were deported. The Holy Land was no more. This was the end of Biblical Judaism: yet again the Jews were wanderers on the face of the earth; they had lost their land and could no longer sacrifice at the Temple. Judaism had radically to rethink its vocation and create for itself, in exile, a new identity.

The Sadducees had tried to prevent this. It used to be thought by scholars that their cooperation with Rome was base collaboration, but this is perhaps unfair judgement. They had the good of Judaism at heart and their policy secured for a while a religious freedom which was remarkable in the empire. Until the revolt the Sadducees controlled the Temple, and the high priest had full power in all matters religious. He could administer the religious law and had the power to exercise the death penalty for religious crimes. Alone among the subjugated people of the empire the Jews did not have to sacrifice to Caesar, something which would have been anathema to their strict monotheism. However, the Sadducees also had personal and less noble reasons for their appeasement of Rome: belonging to the wealthy classes, they had a vested interest in securing their property and privileges; they opposed rebellious elements among their countrymen in order not to rock the boat in which they had a fairly comfortable berth.

The Pharisees were the fierce opponents of the Sadducees in all religious matters, especially the interpretation of the Jewish Law or Torah, which God had given to the Jews on Mount Sinai in the person of Moses. They also had a very different political stance. They were the more popular party, closely identified with the poor, and they controlled Jewish public opinion. They had eventually managed to become included in the Sanhedrin, the religious governing body in Jerusalem, and there worked alongside the Sadducees. The Sadducees, consequently, had to take their opinions into account. To oppose them too much was impossible. 'The people', Josephus tells us, 'would not have it otherwise' (*Antiquitates Judaicae* 18, i, 4). The Pharisees, alongside most of their countrymen, hated the Romans. When bands of Zealot rebels rose up from time to time in Judaea against the Romans their ranks were almost entirely composed of Pharisees. Just after Jesus' birth 2,000 Pharisees were crucified by the Romans for their part in one such uprising. In fact there were very few religious movements in Judaea that were not concerned with the political situation. Even the Essenes, who had withdrawn from the rest of Israel, thinking that Judaism had fallen away from its former ideals, were concerned with politics. They lived austere lives, in a community at Qumran by the Dead Sea. It was almost a monastic existence, but they did not share the indifference to the world that their Christian monastic successors have since practised. Their spirituality was very much part of this world, for most of them joined the Zealots in the great Jewish revolt and were wiped out by the Romans. The land was so closely bound up with the Jewish religion that political indiference was impossible.

From a reading of the gospels you would scarcely know that the Romans were on the scene at all. Apart from a few flattering portraits of centurions, they do not figure much in the story. This is odd, given the political concern of mainstream Judaism during Jesus' lifetime. One Roman, however, does play an important part in the gospel story.

Pontius Pilate arrived in Judaea in about AD 26 when Jesus would have been in his early thirties. He seems to have been one of the most hated of the Roman governors. Philo of Alexandria, whose testimony we should be able to trust, tells us that he was 'naturally inflexible and stubbornly relentless'. Pilate committed 'acts of corruption, insults, rapine, outrages on the people, arrogance, repeated murders of innocent victims and constant and most galling savagery' (*Legatio ad Gaium* 301). Eventually he was recalled to Rome in disgrace, and it is believed that he did not die a natural death. This portrait does not sound much like the Pilate of the gospels; there, far from being inflexible and relentless, he seems a great prevaricator, a weak-minded man who is nevertheless trying to do his best to save Jesus' life. For these pathetic efforts he has been rewarded by canonisation in the Ethiopean church, which regards him as a saint.

The Jewish historian Flavius Josephus tells us the story of Pilate's insult to Judaism which started his term of office in Judaea. It is sometimes difficult to know how far to trust Josephus; an apostate to Rome, he is anxious to flatter the Romans at the same time as presenting his own people in the most becoming light possible, a difficult task at the best of times. His account shows a consequent blurring of details.

The Jewish religion forbade the making of images or statues. Such representations could too easily tempt the Jews into idolatry of the kind practised by the nations surrounding Judaea. The Jews worshipped a spiritual God, who could not be represented adequately by such symbols, but in the early days of Judaism, when monotheism was not so firmly established as it would be later, idolatry was an attraction. The making of graven images was forbidden by the Second Commandment; it was inscribed in the very heart of the Torah. The Romans, who regarded Jewish religious fanaticism warily, did not force images of the emperor on their Jewish subjects – except, Josephus tells us, for Pilate. When he arrived in Judaea he started as he meant to go on, and one night, under cover of darkness, he had the emperor's effigy carried into the sacred precincts of the Temple itself. It was a deliberate insult and provoked an immediate reaction. Thousands of Jews from all over the Holy Land marched to Caesarea where Pilate had his residence. They came in such numbers that they had to be herded into the huge amphitheatre there. Once installed, they flung themselves upon the ground and cried that 'rather would they be killed than break their laws' (*Jewish Wars* 2,9,3). Josephus tells us that Pilate was so impressed that he removed the effigies instantly. Whether or not we choose to believe that Pilate would have been so easily impressed by a race he had just insulted so deeply, some kind of compromise seems to have been reached. But some Jews felt that the sacrilegious presence of graven images in the Temple was the 'abomination of desolation' foretold by the prophet Daniel (Daniel 9: 24), the abomination that would usher in the messianic era.

It was shortly after this that John the Baptist appeared by the river Jordan, urging Israel to accept a baptism of repentence and purification: 'Repent, for the kingdom of God is at hand.'

For the Jew, the phrase 'kingdom of God' had only one meaning. It was not a mystical, divine indwelling of God in the soul of man. It was a kingdom very much of this world. It was the victory of God, foretold by the Prophets, when he would establish his reign on earth. Under the Messiah, he would lead Israel to a cosmic triumph; the gentiles would be vanquished and the messianic era of peace would begin. There would be certain changes in the world. Isaiah had foretold that there would be a transformation of the natural order; wolves would lie down next to lambs, and the child be able to put his hand in the way of a deadly snake without being bitten (Isaiah II: 6 ff.). But for all that it would be an earthly kingdom, Judaism would triumphantly rule the world, administering the reign of God from Jerusalem.

It was a traditional belief that the Messiah would enter Jerusalem in triumph from the Mount of Olives, just outside the city. There was no idea that the Messiah would be anything other than a perfectly normal human being. He might be referred to as the 'son of God' but the Jews' strict monotheism never entertained the possibility that he had a divine nature in the Christian sense. The term 'son of God' could apply to any human being who was specially close to Yahweh, like the king. He would be an ordinary man, beloved by God, and a descendant of King David. He would lead Israel to cosmic triumph over the gentiles.

Jesus claimed to be the Messiah. The gospels tell us that he was secretive about this. He asked his disciples at Caesarea Philippi whom they thought he was and what people were saying about him. There were various speculations, the disciples replied. Some said he was John the Baptist or Elijah returned from the dead. Peter, the leader of the disciples, claimed that Jesus was the 'Messiah, the Son of the Living God' (Matthew 16: 17). Jesus made the disciples promise to keep this to themselves.

Christianity looks back on St Peter's confession and sees in it an assertion of a divine status. Jesus is claiming to be the Son of God, the second person of the blessed Trinity, or rather he is allowing himself to be called this. If these really are Peter's words, however, it is most unlikely that they bear such an interpretation. Jesus calls himself the 'Son of God' or the 'Son of Man' in the synoptic gospels, but only in the Jewish sense. It is not until the Gospel According to St John that he is seen making truly divine claims. In this gospel, the last to be written, the term 'Son of God' has lost its Jewish caution and Jesus can say clearly: 'I and the Father are one' (John 10: 30).

Jesus seems to have started his public life attached to John the Baptist's movement, but after John had been arrested he set up on his own, left the Jordan valley and went north to his native Galilee. At Capernaum he began his mission, and initially his message was the same as John's had been: 'Repent, for the Kingdom of God is at hand.'

How do we know about Jesus? What are our sources?

The earliest Christian writings we possess are the Epistles of St Paul. They were written in the years after AD 50, some twenty years after Jesus' death. The gospels were all written much later. The earliest, that of St Mark, was written in about AD 70, possibly in Rome. Matthew and Luke were written during the 80s by a diaspora Jew and a Greek, and the last gospel, that of St John, was written in about AD 100 in the Middle East. If we take Jesus' death to have occurred in AD 30, which is currently the accepted date, it is clear that all the gospels were written a long time after the events they described and all of them far from the world of Palestinian Judaism, which had been destroyed. In fact the gospels spring out of churches evangelised by St Paul and they reflect much of his teaching. Far from Paul perverting the gospel message, it seems that Paul deeply influenced the evangelists.

The gospels do not purport to be biographies of Jesus, as we in the twentieth century would understand the term. They were all written so long after the event that inevitably oral embellishments crept in and altered the message of Jesus. Scholars are agreed that not all of the words and actions of Jesus recorded in the gospels can be historically true. They have a truth, however. They reflect the way the early Church was thinking about itself in the first century, and the way it saw Jesus; they give evidence of the troubles that Christians were having with the Jews, and they also show a desire to present Christianity in a good light to the

Roman Empire. The concern for historical truth above all else is a modern development. The New Testament writers did not feel themselves bound by historical accuracy, which was, in the circumstances, extremely difficult to guarantee anyway. A lot of the stories and sayings of Jesus recorded in the gospels revolve on the principle of what Jesus would have said were he commenting on later issues such as divorce, the resurrection of the dead or paying tribute to Caesar. There is something refreshing in this approach. After all, the early Church believed that it had the spirit of Jesus and that the spirit would teach them all they needed to know about him. As St John records, Jesus had promised this while he was on earth:

> I have said these things to you while still with you; but the Advocate, the Holy Spirit, whom the Father will send in my name, will teach you everything and remind you of all that I have said to you.

(John 14: 25-26)

This absolute confidence in the spirit is something that later Christianity lost. Much theological writing since has consisted of a dutiful piecing together of texts to produce an argument rather like a patchwork quilt, the texts divorced from their living contexts to be juxtaposed in an attractive but artificial argument. Sometimes the method has been used to justify rather unchristian behaviour, while the gospel methods at least show the truth as something that can continually evolve and change, rather than as a dead collection of severed texts.

Once it has been admitted that the gospels are not historically accurate, that not everything in them is 'gospel truth', where do we draw the line? It is possible to sift through the later mythologising and additions and get some idea of what actually happened, but it is a complicated procedure and certainty cannot be guaranteed.

What kind of Messiah was Jesus claiming to be? Later

Christianity would present him as coming down to earth to save the world, but the Jews were expecting a Messiah who came only for the Jews. It seems clear that Jesus preached only to the Jews; the later idea that his mission was also for the gentiles was, as we shall see, wholly due to Paul.

Judaism had no real missionary sense; it could not have, as it was a religion founded on race. If you were not born a Jew you could not belong to the 'chosen people', and that was that. In the diaspora many gentiles and Greeks were drawn to Judaism and become honorary members of the synagogues. A very few were circumcised, but most balked at this and followed Judaism from a distance. These converts were known as the 'Godfearers' and were tolerated, even welcomed, but they were always ultimately outsiders.

Jesus probably shared this Jewish exclusivism. In Capernaum he taught in the synagogues as an ordinary young rabbi, and throughout his career there is no indication that he sought out gentiles or tried to win them over. His doctrine of the kingdom was entirely Jewish – there had never been a tradition that the Messiah would start a new religion. At the Last Supper, Jesus is reported to have said that he was instituting a 'new covenant', which sounds a radical departure. But the very use of the word 'covenant' is so Jewish that it cannot be inferred that Jesus wanted to break away from Judaism. The Essenes too had their own covenant, but they never considered themselves separated from the original covenant with Abraham. On the contrary, as we have seen, they valued Judaism enough to die for it in the great Jewish revolt.

There is one gospel story which indicates that, far from going out to seek the gentiles, Jesus actually disliked them, with typical Jewish contempt. When a Syro-Phoenician woman asked him for help he tastelessly snapped: 'It is not fair to take the children's food and throw it to the dogs.' Admittedly he did help her in the end, but only after she admitted her inferior status: 'Yes sir, but even the dogs can eat the scraps that fall from the Master's table' (Matthew 15: 21-28). Perhaps this incident never happened, but even if Jesus never said the words 'I was sent only to the lost sheep of the House of Israel' (Matthew 15: 25), it is certainly true that his first followers, unlike the vast majority of Christians today, were Jewish. His first Apostles – Peter and Andrew, James and John – were all Jewish.

But surely if Jesus was only preaching to Jews, the content of his message was something completely new? It seems uncertain that this is the case. In the gospels, Jesus is represented as an entirely original teacher, whose doctrines were rejected by the Jews of his time – particularly by the Pharisees – because Judaism had lost all spirituality in a mechanical following of the letter of the Law and a neglect of its spirit. The Pharisees are the real villains of the gospel story and a most unpleasant picture emerges from Jesus' constant denunciations. They are hypocrites, they spend their time showing off their virtue and quibbling about the minutiae of the observance of the Law of Moses:

> Then addressing the people and his disciples Jesus said, 'The scribes and the Pharisees occupy the chair of Moses. You must therefore do what they tell you and listen to what they say, but do not be guided by what they do: since they do not practise what they preach. They tie up heavy burdens and lay them on men's shoulders, but will they lift a finger to move them? Not they! Everything they do is done to attract attention, like wearing broader phylacteries and longer tassels, like wanting to take the place of honour at banquets and the front seat in the synagogues, being greeted obsequiously in the market squares and having people call them Rabbi.'
>
> (Matthew 23: 1-7)

Throughout the gospels, the Pharisees try to catch Jesus out. They challenge him particularly about points of sabbath observance, especially because he insists on healing people on the sabbath. They care obsessively about matters of ritual purity, and their inflexible legalism involves them in endless hypocrisy:

> 'Alas for you, scribes and Pharisees, you hypocrites! You who clean the outside of the cup and dish and leave the inside full of extortion and intemperance. Blind Pharisee! Clean the inside of the cup and dish first so that the outside may become clean as well.
>
> 'Alas for you, scribes and Pharisees, you hypocrites! You who are like whitewashed tombs that look handsome on the outside, but inside are full of dead men's bones and every kind of corruption. In the same way you appear to people from the outside like good, honest men, but inside you are full of hypocrisy and lawlessness.
>
> 'Alas for you, scribes and Pharisees, you hypocrites! You who build the sepulchres of the prophets and decorate the tombs of holy men, saying: "We would never have joined in shedding the blood of the prophets, had we lived in our fathers' day." So! Your own evidence tells against you! You are the sons of those who murdered the prophets! Very well then, finish off the work that your fathers began.'

(Matthew 23: 25-32)

It is the Pharisees and the scribes, the scholars of the synagogues, who will ultimately be responsible for Jesus' own death, as he tells them in this passage. They are leading their fellow Jews astray, because they have lost all sense of the spirit of their religion. It is Jesus' mission in life to rectify this, to bring back a religion based on the heart and filled with love, instead of a hypocritical and mechanical concern with externals.

This portrait of the Pharisees is accepted by most Christians without question, but sometimes a feeling of disquiet creeps in as we read Jesus' swingeing denunciations. What has happened to his teaching 'love your enemies'? Jesus tells his disciples: 'Do not judge . . . Why do you observe the splinter in your brother's eye and never notice the plank in your own' (Matthew 7: 1-3). It seems that he is not setting a very good example to his followers in his scathing judgements. Also, who were all these prophets that the fathers of the Pharisees are supposed to have killed? It is difficult to find in the Old Testament an example of even one murder of a prophet, let alone the massacres that Jesus refers to.

It has long been recognised that the gospel portrait of the Pharisees is a distortion. The picture of a complacent group of religious hypocrites delighted with their good deeds and concerned only with an arid observance of the Law has little basis in fact. When we turn to the writings of the rabbis and Pharisees at about this time, we find that far from opposing their teaching in every respect, Jesus seems to have taught much the same as they did. The more we read of the rabbis, the more we see that Jesus' teaching is for the most part well within the rabbinic traditions and not strikingly original. Like the Pharisees, he is insistent that 'Charity and deeds of loving kindness are equal to all the *mitzvot* in the Torah' (Tosefta Peah 4: 19). Like the Pharisees too he teaches in parables. There is one Pharisaic parable, for example, that closely resembles Jesus' parable of the prodigal son:

> 'Thou wilt return to the Lord thy God.'[1] R. Samuel Pargrita said in the name of Rabbi Meir: This can be compared to the son of a king who took to evil ways. The king sent a tutor to him, saying, 'Repent, my son.' The son, however, sent him back to his father (with a message). 'How can I have the effrontery to return? I am ashamed to come before you.' Thereupon his father sent back word, 'My son, is a son ever ashamed to return to his father? And it is not to your father that you will be returning?' Similarly the Holy one, Blessed be He, sent Jeremiah to Israel when they sinned.
>
> (Deuteronomy Rabbah 2: 24)

Like the Pharisees, Jesus teaches his followers about a God who is a loving father and always ready to forgive his erring children. Like the Pharisee Rabbi Hillel, arguably the

1. Deuteronomy 4: 30.

greatest Pharisee of them all, Jesus teaches a version of the 'golden rule': 'So always treat others as you would like them to treat you. This is the meaning of the Law and the Prophets' (Matthew 7: 12).

> On another occasion it happened that a certain heathen came before Shammai and said to him, 'Make me a proselyte on condition that you teach me the whole Torah while I stand on one foot.' Thereupon he repulsed him with a builder's cubit which was in his hand. When he went before Hillel, he said to him, 'What is hateful to you do not to your neigh-bour; that is the whole Torah and all the rest is commentary thereof. Go and learn it.'
>
> (Shabbath 31a)

Sometimes Jesus almost sounds like a Pharisee himself. The Pharisees too were concerned to sum up the Torah in one or two commandments, not multiply new *mitzvot*. Hillel summed it up, like Jesus, with the golden rule. Rabbi Nahaman ben Isaac based the whole Torah on the words of Habbakuk 2: 4: 'But the righteous shall live by his faith' (R. Simlai on Makkoth 24a). Similarly Jesus as a young rabbi was approached often and asked how he would sum up the Torah:

> One of the scribes who had listened to them debating and had observed how well Jesus had answered them, now came up and put a question to him, 'Which is the first of all the commandments?' Jesus replied, 'This is the first: *Listen Israel, the Lord our God is one Lord, and you must love the Lord your God with all your heart, with all your soul,*[1] with all your mind, and *with all your strength.*[2] The second is this: *You must love your neighbour as yourself.*[3] There is no commandment greater than these.' The scribe said to him, 'Well spoken, Master; what you have said is true: that he is one and there is no other. To love him with all your heart,

1. Deuteronomy 6: 4-5.
2. Deuteronomy 6: 5.
3. Leviticus 19: 18.

with all your understanding and strength, and to love your neighbour as yourself, this is far more important than any holocaust or sacrifice.' Jesus, seeing how wisely he had spoken, said, 'You are not far from the kingdom of God.' After that no one dared to question him any more.

(Mark 12: 28-34)

The endless disputes or debates with the Pharisees and scribes, who often want to catch Jesus out, probably have a foundation in fact. The Pharisees' studies were not conducted in libraries, but publicly by means of discussion and often lively and contentious argument. You can still see this principle today in a rabbinic *yeshivah*. Like an ordinary rabbi, Jesus would be judged by his skill in debate, and would impress people by his wisdom and by the use of scripture, just as he impresses the scribe here. It is noteworthy too that when he is asked to sum up his teaching, he does so in two quotations from the Old Testament. The first quotation from Deuteronomy 6: 4-5 is the great *shema*, the Jewish confession of faith which is publicly recited on the sabbath. Far from wishing to lead his followers away from Judaism, he is seen as teaching well within its traditions, and within the traditions of the Pharisees who are supposedly his enemies.

Paul, we have seen, writes proudly of having been a Pharisee before his conversion, which he would hardly have done if they had been Jesus' sworn enemies and had hounded him to his death. Luke, the evangelist who is closest to Paul in spirit, is also quite pro-Pharisee in his gospel and in Acts of the Apostles. But when we turn to the gospels of Matthew and John we find an anti-semitism that is distressing; the worst casualties are the Pharisees.

Even the anti-semitic Matthew has Jesus say in the Sermon on the Mount: 'Do you think that I have come to set aside the Law and the Prophets, I have not come to set them aside but to bring them to perfection' (5: 17). Matthew and John were writing long after the destruction of Jerusalem and were ignorant about Palestinian Judaism; either they did not understand what the Pharisees were teaching or they wished to present Judaism in a bad light. No Pharisee, for example, would ever have objected to Jesus' healing on the sabbath. It had always been possible to heal on the sabbath; the Talmud expressly made allowance for this. Admittedly the evangelists were not recording the exact words of Jesus, but the tenor of his teachings seems remarkably close to the rabbinic writings. Their only originality lies in the fact that the evangelists had a greater literary talent to express it poetically.

One of the first followers of Jesus was Matthew (sometimes called Levi), a tax collector. Tax collectors were considered the lowest of the low. Any Jew who could so collaborate with the Romans that he was willing to collect their hated taxes from his fellow Jews was shunned as though he had a contagious disease. Nobody would eat with him or consort with him in case his treachery and sinful collaboration was passed on. Collaborators and tax collectors are called 'publicans' and 'sinners' in the gospels. Jesus went out of his way to convert these 'sick' people to a stronger sense of their Jewish vocation. Throughout his career he consorted with them, ate with them, and was friendly with them. This caused a certain amount of scandal. After his conversion, Levi had a party for Jesus:

> In his honour Levi held a great reception in his house and with them at table was a large gathering of tax collectors and others. The Pharisees and their scribes complained to his disciples and said, 'Why do you eat and drink with tax collectors and sinners?' Jesus said to them in reply, 'It is not those who are well who need a physician but the sick. I have not come to call the virtuous, but sinners, to repentance.'
> (Luke 5: 29-32)

Because 'tax collector' has for centuries been translated as 'publican', the general impression has arisen that Jesus went out of his way to consort with the loose-livers of Israel in pubs and taverns. This view is strengthened by Jesus' converting and championing prostitutes like Mary Magdalen, and mixing with 'sinners', the morally weak. This is a misconception. We are using the word 'sinner' here with its Christian connotations, connotations which we shall see it got from St Paul. The Jews did not have a sense of sin comparable to the Christian sense: 'sinner' for the Jew did not mean what it would mean later in Paul's writings, but was the term for a collaborator. When the Pharisees ask Jesus what he is doing consorting with 'sinners' they are not showing an uncharitable attitude to people who are living immoral lives. If they had condemned Jesus for that, they would truly be the complacent group Christians have always considered them, thinking their own virtue so impregnable that they need have nothing to do with anyone who did not come up to their high standards. What the anti-Roman Pharisees were surprised about was that Jesus was consorting with the collaborators who were betraying their race and religion. Mary Magdalen was a 'sinner' not only because she was a prostitute; she probably also slept with the Roman soldiers. Jesus' reply is that they (the Pharisees) do not need him. They understand their Jewish vocation. The kingdom of God is coming, and Israel must be purged of her 'sickness'. That is why he is so concerned with the 'sinners', also called the 'sick'. They need to be cured, before the kingdom is established, so that Israel is worthy.

Jesus acquired a large following in Galilee. One of the reasons for his popularity was his astonishing success as a faith healer. Like his concern for the 'sick' of Israel, his miracles of healing are an essential part of his messianic claim. When the kingdom of God comes it will sweep away all obstacles, physical, spiritual or political, and the power residing in Jesus to heal is a foretaste of the power of God in the messianic era.

Eventually Jesus left Galilee and went to Jerusalem. From that moment the gospels become very confused and full of contradictions. On the one hand Jesus says that in going to Jerusalem he is deliberately courting death; he knows that the Jews are hostile to him. He repeatedly prophesies his Passion in detail:

> From that time Jesus began to make it clear to his disciples that he was destined to go to Jerusalem and suffer grievously at the hands of the elders and chief priests and scribes, to be put to death and to be raised up on the third day. Then taking him aside, Peter started to remonstrate with him. 'Heaven preserve you, Lord,' he said, 'this must not happen to you.' But he turned and said to Peter, 'Get behind me, Satan! You are an obstacle in my path, because the way you think is not God's way but man's.'

(Matthew 16: 21-23)

Yet despite these unmistakable prophecies which are ultimately hopeful – Jesus will rise again on the third day – the Crucifixion comes as a terrible shock to the disciples. They seem not to have expected it at all. Instead of waiting hopefully for the resurrection, or even the off-chance of the resurrection, they scattered and fled – the news that Jesus had in fact risen from the dead came as a complete surprise. In St John's gospel it seems that they had even gone home to Galilee and back to their old occupations, abandoning Jesus as a lost cause.

A second major contradiction is that Jesus stated that he was to suffer at the hands of the Jews, and yet he died by the Roman punishment of crucifixion. In St John's gospel, when Pilate tells the Jews to 'Take him yourselves, and try him by your own Law', the Jews reply, 'We are not allowed to put a man to death' (John 18: 31). This shows a complete ignorance of the true state of affairs in Jerusalem. The Sanhedrin had full power to administer the death sentence in religious matters. They would not crucify a man, as they abominated crucifixion. Stoning was the death penalty for blasphemy, and the gospels say that this was Jesus' offence: he claimed to be the Son of God. As a further complication, we have seen that except in St John's gospel there is nothing blasphemous about this claim; if Jesus claimed to be the Messiah this involved no blasphemy. In Acts of the Apostles, Luke preserves for us the typical Pharisaic response to such claims: let's wait and see. When the Apostles were summoned before the Sanhedrin for their preaching about the risen Messiah this is what happened:

> One member of the Sanhedrin, however, a Pharisee called Gamaliel, who was a doctor of the Law and respected by the whole people, stood up and asked to have the men taken outside for a while. Then he addressed the Sanhedrin, 'Men of Israel, be careful how you deal with these people. There was Theudas who became notorious not so long ago. He claimed to be someone important, and he even collected about four hundred followers; but when he was killed, all his followers scattered and that was the end of them. And then there was Judas the Galilean, at the time of the census, who attracted crowds of supporters; but he got killed too, and all his followers dispersed. What I suggest, therefore, is that you leave these men alone and let them go. If this enterprise, this movement of theirs, is of human origin it will break up of its own accord; but if it does in fact come from God you will not only be unable to destroy them, but you might find yourself fighting God.'

(Acts 5: 34-39)

Luke has got his dates badly confused here but this does not alter the basic attitude. Where was Gamaliel and his advice · on the night of Jesus' trial before the Sanhedrin?

What really happened and why did Jesus die by the Roman death of crucifixion? Many answers have been suggested but it is unlikely that we shall ever be certain. No self-respecting Pharisee would hand a fellow Jew to the hated Romans. It has been said that the Sadducees would have worried about Jesus' claim to be the Messiah, the 'King of Israel', because this could create danger for the Jewish nation with the Romans, who certainly would tolerate no such claim. Other scholars have suggested that the trial before the Sanhedrin was an attempt to save Jesus' life. What the gospels are unanimous about is that it was the Jews who were responsible for Jesus' death, in retrospect most unlikely and a reflection on first-century anti-semitism.

Jesus began by entering Jerusalem in triumph and the procession seems to have been some kind of messianic statement. He began his journey on the Mount of Olives, whence the Messiah was supposed to arrive. He also came riding on an ass in fulfilment of Zechariah's prophecy:

> Say to the daughter of Zion: Look, your king comes to you; he is humble, he rides on a donkey and on a colt, the foal of a beast of burden.
>
> (Zechariah 9: 9)

He had a most enthusiastic welcome. Crowds rushed forward to greet him, spreading garments and branches in his path and shouting, 'Hosannah to the Son of David.' The word *hosannah* means 'save us' or 'liberate us'. The Messiah was to be the descendant of David, the king who had established the first free Jewish kingdom in Jerusalem, which he captured from the Jebusites.

Was this public enthusiasm inspired solely by Jesus' spiritual teaching? If it was, the crowds appear to have grasped remarkably little of its essence, since a few days later they were howling for his death. It is more likely that there was some kind of political as well as messianic claim being made by Jesus when he entered Jerusalem. What kind of Messiah was he claiming to be? It was once customary to assert that Jesus was a Zealot who was threatening the Romans with a military *coup*, but that view has little support these days. It may have been that he was claiming a more pacific victory based on prayer and miracle, rather than a show of military strength. It may even be that he was not predominantly interested in politics, but was founding a more spiritual Jewish 'covenant' within Israel. Yet any messianic claim had to deal somehow with the gentiles, and some political stance was inevitable in Judaism at that time. Whatever kind of Messiah Jesus was claiming to be, he died by Roman punishment, and on his cross was written 'King of the Jews'.

The gospel account of Pilate ill-accords with what we know about him from other sources. The gospels are adamant that Pilate tried to save Jesus' life and that it was the Jews who insisted, howled at Pilate and threatened him, bullying him into condemning Jesus, but the story does not hold water. There is no record of any custom that the Roman governor released a prisoner on the feast of Passover, so the Barabbas story is dubious. No Roman governor, let alone Pilate, would have spent a morning trying to save the life of a Galilean upstart. No governor of any time would have conducted a trial by leaping in and out of his courtroom to plead with the barbarous natives, including an impertinent group who refused to enter his house in case they were contaminated. To save the life of anyone who claimed to be king of the Jews – in whatever sense – was more than Pilate's own life was worth. Tiberias had had people summarily executed for less. Finally, no Jew would have howled for the death of one of their number at the hands of the hated Romans.

The gospels claim that Jesus' arrest had to be at night and conducted in the deepest secrecy, because of his great popularity with the people. So who were these Jews who were outside the prison that morning? It was the morning of Passover, which involved immense preparations, yet there was apparently a whole mob with nothing better to do than wait around outside the prison on the off-chance that Pilate was going to be too lenient with one of his prisoners and might need their presence. Matthew claims that when Pilate pleaded Jesus' innocence, and washed his hands of this man's blood, they cried, 'His blood be upon us and upon our children' (27: 26). This is the highly improbable sentence on which Christian anti-semitism – and there has been a good deal of it – is based.

At all events, Jesus was taken outside the city to a hill called Golgotha and there, in the company of two other criminals, Pilate's sentence was carried out. How did he view his death? Did he see it as the first step in his glorious triumph, a death which would save the world? Or did he view it as the failure of his messianic bid? Why, just before he was arrested, when his death appeared inevitable, did he pray in an agony in the garden of Gethsemane, so that the sweat poured off him like large drops of blood? What did his death mean to him that he cried from the cross: 'My God, my God, why hast thou forsaken me?' (Mark 15: 34).

What would Jesus' death mean to Paul?

2 Paul's conversion

The death and resurrection of Jesus came to be crucially important to Paul. For him these events changed the whole course of human history. We shall see that it was most important to him that Jesus' death was a matter of historical fact, not a mere myth or legend.

Was Paul fully aware of the actual circumstances of Jesus' death? It seems almost certain that he was, although he was not involved at all with Jesus during his lifetime. We cannot even be sure that he was in Judaea during Jesus' mission and at the time of his death. Luke tells us, in Acts of the Apostles, that Paul had studied the Torah in Jerusalem under the famous Rabbi Gamaliel. Paul never mentions this, which has led some scholars to doubt the connection with Gamaliel. Nevertheless Paul was a Pharisee before his conversion, and would almost certainly have studied in Judaea. When he writes to the Philippians about his Pharisaism, perhaps he does not mention Gamaliel because Christian converts in far-off Macedonia would not have heard of the Jewish scholar. He does say in Galatians that for years after his conversion he was 'unknown by sight to the churches of Christ in Judaea' (1:22), which some scholars have taken to mean that he was not in Jerusalem before his conversion, though Paul could well have studied in Jerusalem without making the acquaintance of a crowd of Galileans headed by a teacher of whom he disapproved.

Paul was not involved in Jesus' life or in the events that led to his death. At that time he had other concerns, notably the study of the Torah. Even after his conversion, Jesus' earthly life does not seem to have interested Paul at all. In his Epistles he never tells stories about Jesus, nor does he, apart from a few rare occasions, quote any of the teachings that Jesus made while on earth. Rather, he makes a point of not doing so. Later he had to defend his authority as an apostle, one who had a mission to preach the gospel, against the claims of those who had personally known Jesus, who enjoyed *kudos* in the early Church. Paul had no time for people who claimed seniority on such grounds. In his writings he defiantly claims full equality with them and asserts the authority and supremacy of his own revelation, sweeping aside as irrelevant others' claims to have been friends of the earthly Jesus: 'Even if we did know Jesus Christ according to the flesh, that is not how we know him any longer' (2 Corinthians 5:16).

For all this, it is likely that Paul was aware of the events of Jesus' life, probably more so than the later evangelists and certainly more than modern scholars or Christians are today, simply because he was so much closer in time and place to the events. He knew enough about Jesus to persecute his first followers:

> You must have heard of my career as a practising Jew, how merciless I was in persecuting the Church of God, how much damage I did to it, how I stood out among other Jews of my generation, and how enthusiastic I was for the traditions of my ancestors . . .

he writes to the Galatians (1:13-14). It may have been that for him the concept of a crucified Messiah was scandalous. Later he writes that to the Jews the Cross of Christ is a 'stumbling block', 'an obstacle that they cannot get over' (1 Corinthians 1:23)

Luke claims that Paul had authority from the high priest to round up the followers of Jesus in Damascus, though it is difficult to see how Paul, a Pharisee could have been willing to join forces with the rival party. However, we know that Paul would have differed radically from the other Pharisees in his view of the Roman Empire, which he supported throughout his life: he was only a Pharisee 'as for the Law' (Philippians 3:6). The Sadducees probably regarded Jesus' claim to be king of the Jews, and the subsequent claims of his disciples that he was the Messiah who had risen gloriously from the dead, as politically dangerous. Whatever his reasons, Paul was at first fiercely opposed to the early Church and persecuted it with characteristic single-minded enthusiasm. There is an interesting phrase in Paul's account of himself as a persecutor. He 'stood out', he says, 'among the other Jews of my generation' in this respect. The obvious meaning of this is that Paul's attitude to Jesus was exemplary, but it could also mean that it was unusual. It is perhaps true that at first not many other Jews thought that there was anything much the matter with this new religious movement. On the contrary – Jesus had wanted to remain within Judaism and so did his first followers.

Our sources are no longer the gospels, of course, which finish their accounts with Jesus' resurrection. Our knowledge of the subsequent events and the history of the early Church are Paul's Epistles and Acts of the Apostles, traditionally ascribed to St Luke. Paul's letters are the earliest Christian writings. They were composed in a short space of time about twenty years after Jesus' death. However, not all the Epistles ascribed to Paul in the New Testament were actually written by him. The Epistle to the Hebrews certainly was not, neither were the 'pastoral' Epistles to Timothy and Titus. Many scholars are dubious about Colossians and even more doubt the authenticity of Ephesians, which could have been written as late as AD 100. The second letter to the Thessalonians is probably not Paul's. We are left with 1 Thessalonians, 1 and 2 Corinthians, Galatians, Philippians, Romans and Philemon. This does not mean that people were trying to pull off elaborate forgeries. The other Pauline Epistles were written sometimes years after Paul's death by his followers who formed a Pauline school. To write in the *persona* of the master was at that time a common way of expressing discipleship.

Paul's letters are partisan; he shamelessly and vehemently presents only his own view. But in the Epistles we often find things that completely contradict Luke in Acts of the Apostles. Luke too is partisan. He is a great admirer of Paul and has absorbed many of his ideas, but he also has other objectives which often make him present 'facts' in as biased a way as Paul does. Acts was written at the end of the first century – again, long after the events described. It finishes with Paul's arrival in Rome, which probably took place in the early 60s. Luke has several aims. He is writing some twenty years after the great Jewish revolt and, like his master, Paul, he is an admirer of the Roman Empire. In their revolt the Jews had managed to hold the mighty Roman army at bay for four years and, with extraordinary tenacity, inflicted on Rome immense casualties and loss of life. Jews were, therefore, by the time Luke was writing, not in good odour among the Roman authorities. Luke is at pains to show that, from the very first, the Church was on increasingly bad terms with the Jews and on excellent terms with the Romans. The Romans are presented as exemplary. They are deeply impressed by Paul and his preaching, even if they have to imprison him occasionally, whereas the Jews started persecuting the Church very early. Another objective of Luke is to show that from the start the Church was strongly united; there were no disputes, no differences of opinion. He presents an idyllic view of Christian life, with the Christians living together in loving brotherhood, holding possessions in common, a portrait probably based on ideals of Christian behaviour current at the end of the first century. Paul's letters show quite a different picture; even

Luke's narrative sometimes cracks slightly – discrepancies occur which show that everything was not as peaceful as he makes out.

Acts is beautifully written, but in some ways it presents the crudest picture of Christianity in the New Testament. It has been called the 'gospel of the holy spirit' and certainly the charismatic is much in evidence. Miracles abound, but unlike the miracles of Jesus they are not always of healing. The miracles are sometimes an expression of divine brute force, which show the God of Paul to be stronger than the gods or powers of rival magicians. People are struck blind, struck dead. There is a strongly fictional flavour at times. Also, with the usual freedom of New Testament writers, if Luke is not quite sure what happened he will cheerfully make something up.

Again, this is not to say that Luke is telling lies. Like the gospel accounts of Jesus' life, Luke's stories certainly have a truth even if they are not always historically accurate. They express the truth of an ideal or a theology; they make a different point from the purely historical one and often the point may be a valid one about Paul or about the Church.

It was three or four years after Jesus' death before Paul was converted to belief in Jesus. By that time Jesus' first followers had had a chance to establish themselves along their own lines, before Paul's tumultuous presence challenged some of their deepest beliefs. The first members of the Church were not Christians as we use the term today. In fact it was not until Paul's historic conversion on the road to Damascus that Christianity, as we know it, was born.

Jesus was a Jew; so were his first followers; like Jesus they preached only to other Jews. It seems likely from recent archaeological evidence that an early meeting place for these first Jewish Christians was on Mount Zion in Jerusalem. This is in itself interesting. Mount Zion marked the site of the ancient citadel captured by King David from the Jebusites when he established the first Jewish kingdom in

Jerusalem. On Mount Zion, beneath the beautiful Crusader building which marks the site of the 'cenacle' or the 'upper room' mentioned in the gospels as the first Christian meeting place, is also the traditional site of the tomb of David. This is symbolic of the belief of the Jewish Christians. It was in the upper room that Jesus celebrated the Last Supper; it was in the upper room that he appeared to his disciples after his resurrection, and it was here that the apostles received the holy spirit and thence rushed into Jerusalem to begin preaching. Christians come to Mount Zion to pray at the birthplace of Christianity. Certainly they can pray at a place that was important to Jesus, but Mount Zion is, strictly, the birthplace of a Jewish sect which sought only to remain within Judaism and did not intend to found a new religion.

Beneath the cenacle, Jews still pray at the tomb of David, their national hero. The Messiah was to be a son of David and Jesus of Nazareth was hailed as such when he rode in triumph into Jerusalem. Underlying the faith of his first followers, the Jewish Christians, who quite soon became known as the Nazarenes after their founder, was a belief in Jesus as a Jewish Messiah, who like King David would establish the kingdom of God in Jerusalem. He had risen from the dead and appeared to the apostles. He had promised that he would return in glory to establish God's kingdom, which would mean the ultimate triumph of the Jews over the gentiles. In Acts, Luke tells us that the Jewish Christians 'went as a body to the Temple every day' (2: 46). No gentiles were allowed within the Temple's sacred precincts, and there was no reason why the Nazarenes should have been interested in preaching to the gentiles: Jesus would come back to establish the power of God over the gentiles; they would be vanquished, not saved.

In Acts we learn that a number of the new converts to Jesus were Pharisees (15: 5) and this included their leader, James, Jesus' brother, who became know as James the Just.

James was stoned to death by the Sadducees in AD 62 in what appears to have been a purely Jewish quarrel. When he was condemned, eighty Pharisees protested to the Sanhedrin on his behalf and died with him. This is an important point. Christianity today sees itself as a religion that is quite separate from Judaism; the New Testament says that the Jews rejected Christ, had him killed, and persecuted his early followers. They lost their chance of salvation because they would not recognise that he was the Messiah, that he was God. However, the very first Jewish Christians wanted to stay within Judaism. That Christianity is now a separate religion is due ultimately to Paul. The only thing that distinguished adherents of the first Church in Jerusalem from their fellow Jews was their belief that Jesus was the Messiah – which, as we have seen from Gamaliel's argument to the Sanhedrin in Acts, was a far from unorthodox position. It might be unusual to preach about a Messiah who had been crucified, but the Pharisaic attitude was to wait and see; time would tell. Neither to James the Just nor to the Pharisees who died with him was there any incompatibility between Judaism and the belief that Jesus was the long-expected Messiah.

However, quite early there was a division in the ranks and it is here that Paul makes his first appearance in the Christian story, although not everyone is convinced that the incident is entirely historical. Among the first followers of Jesus who were converted by the apostles' teaching were a number of Jews and 'Godfearers' from the diaspora, whom Acts calls Hellenists or 'those who speak Greek' (6: 1). That there was tension between the Hellenists and the Judaic Jewish Christians is indicated when Luke says that 'the Hellenists made a complaint against the Hebrews: in the daily distribution their own widows were being overlooked (Acts 6: 1). In his efforts to present a picture of a solidly united Church, Luke records that the dispute was quickly resolved by instituting seven deacons to look after the administration. The succeeding incident in Acts shows that the source of the trouble could have been connected with deeper issues and the division was of longer duration.

The preaching of some of these Hellenists in the Temple, in particular the preaching of one Stephen, so enraged other Jews that there were riots and Stephen was killed by stoning. Since stoning was the traditional Jewish punishment for blasphemy, one can only speculate as to what in Stephen's preaching the Jews considered blasphemous. The 'false witnesses' against Stephen in Acts claim that 'This man is always making speeches against this Holy Place and the Law. We have heard him say that Jesus the Nazarene is going to destroy this Place and alter the traditions that Moses handed down to us' (6: 13-14). In his final speech Stephen denounced Jews and Judaism. If Luke is correct, this would have been both blasphemy and a radical departure for the new movement, causing a split in the early Christian ranks. On the day of Stephen's death, Luke says, 'a bitter persecution started against the church in Jerusalem, and everyone except the apostles fled to the country districts of Judaea and Samaria' (Acts 8: 1) – Judaism had started violently to reject Christianity. And yet one phrase is revealing: 'except the apostles'. It is an odd sort of persecution which ignores the ringleaders of a sect and attacks only their followers. It is far more likely that the Hellenist Jews, who are later (Acts 11: 18) discovered to have fled to the diaspora and who established churches there, were the culprits. There may have been something in their belief which was antagonistic to Judaic faith, whereas the 'apostles' who remained in Jerusalem were considered orthodox.

Luke's account of Stephen's death is most edifying, and seems very similar to the death of Jesus; he dies forgiving his persecutors. Also present was a young man called Saul:

> But Stephen, filled with the Holy Spirit, gazed into Heaven and saw the glory of God, and Jesus standing at God's right hand. 'I can see Heaven thrown open,' he said, 'and the Son

of Man standing at the right hand of God.' At this all the members of the council shouted out and stopped their ears with their hands; then they all rushed at him, sent him out of the city and stoned him. The witnesses put down their clothes at the feet of a young man named Saul. As they were stoning him, Stephen said in invocation, 'Lord Jesus, receive my spirit.' Then he knelt down and said aloud, 'Lord do not hold this sin against them'; and with these words he fell asleep. Saul entirely approved of the killing.

(Acts 7: 55-8: 1)

The last sentence is true in a sense. Paul (his Jewish name was Saul, Paul was his Roman name) would certainly have approved, but many scholars doubt the actual presence of Paul at Stephen's martyrdom, maintaining that at this point he was 'unknown by sight to any of the Churches in Judaea' (Galatians 1: 22), and this would not have been the case if he had played an important part at Stephen's martyrdom. Whether Paul was historically there or not, there is a symbolic truth in his presence on the scene. Luke implies that Stephen rejected the Temple ritual and the Law of Moses, just as Paul would do later. Also after this persecution, the diaspora Christians fled from Judaea. We next hear of them establishing a church in Antioch (Acts 11: 18), and at Antioch Paul established himself firmly later in his career. There was a link, in Luke's mind, between Paul and Stephen.

What happened to transform Paul from an ardent persecutor of the Church into a zealous follower of Jesus? For some time scholars thought that Paul became increasingly dissatisfied with Judaism, that he found the huge demands of the Law impossible and that this induced in him a crippling guilt and sense of spiritual impotence. In his letter to the Romans he wrote, years after this, in terms that could suggest this to the unwary reader:

What I mean is that I should not have known what sin was except for the Law. I should not for instance have known what it means to covet if the Law had not said *You shall not covet*[1] But this commandment sin took advantage of to produce all kinds of covetousness in me, for when there is no Law sin is dead.

Once when there was no Law I was alive; but when the commandment came, sin came to life and I died; the commandment was meant to lead me to life but it turned out to mean death to me . . .

The Law, of course, as we all know, is spiritual: but I am unspiritual; I have been sold as a slave to sin. I cannot understand my own behaviour. I fail to carry out the things I want to do, and I find myself doing the very things that I hate.

(Romans 7: 7-10, 14-14)

Seeing these verses in the context of the whole letter makes it clear that this passage is not autobiographical. When Paul uses the pronoun 'I' in this instance, he is not referring to himself personally, but writing in the person of the whole of unredeemed mankind. Without Christ, Paul came to see later, all men were in this state, even Jews who had been given the immense privilege of the Law. All men are slaves of sin. Yet before his conversion there is no hint that Paul was anything but committed to Judaism. Instead of being guilt-ridden, he writes that he was 'faultless' in his observance of the Law and an exemplary Jew (Philippians 3: 6).

Paul's was not an easy conversion; it was not a gradual intellectual approach to a new faith, a process of worrying disillusion, dawning light and a final glad commitment. It was not a spiritual odyssey of the sort we have become accustomed to in the lives of Cardinal Newman or Ronald Knox. Paul himself refers to it always as a 'revelation' – a vision: 'The good news I preached is not a human message that I was given by men, it is something I learnt only through a revelation of Jesus Christ' (Galatian 1: 11). Luke shows us that, far from being a process of rational enlighten-

1. Exodus 20: 17.

ment and natural searching, the vision literally struck him down while he was on a mission of persecution to punish the followers of Jesus in Damascus. It is one of the most dramatic conversions the world has known. Right up to the last second before his vision, Paul was a deeply committed Jew entirely antagonistic to the new faith:

> Meanwhile Saul was still breathing threats to slaughter the Lord's disciples. He had gone to the High Priest and asked for letters addressed to the synagogues in Damascus, that they would authorise him to arrest and take to Jerusalem any followers of the Way, men or women, that he could find.
>
> Suddenly, while he was travelling to Damascas and just before he reached the city, there came a light from heaven all round him. He fell to the ground and then he heard a voice saying, 'Saul, Saul, Why are you persecuting me?' 'Who are you, Lord?' he asked, and the voice answered, 'I am Jesus, and you are persecuting me. Get up now and go into the city and you will be told what you have to do.' The men travelling with Saul stood there speechless, for though they heard the voice, they could see no one. Saul got up from the ground but even with his eyes wide open he could see nothing at all, and they had to lead him into Damascas by hand.

(Acts 9: 1-9)

Paul's vision is not unique; nor is the transcendental experience limited to Christianity. Throughout history men and women have had similar visions and been impelled by them to acts of supreme courage and endurance. It is the same kind of experience that Wordsworth described, when,

> the light of sense
> Goes out, but with a flash that has revealed
> the invisible world.

(*The Prelude* VI, 600-602)

Ordinary, mundane reality is blotted out in an intense moment of new perception, which transcends facts and reason. A similar kind of experience sends epileptics, like Dostoevski's Idiot, into an ecstatic convulsion of mind and body, or it can thrust the schizophrenic into a hell which the 'real' world cannot penetrate. Sometimes the results can be startling. Relatively recently Theresa Neuman and Pio Nono, had such an intense experience of the Passion of Christ that they physically reproduced in themselves the five wounds that bled with horrible realism. In 1913 three illiterate children at Fatima so believed in their own vision of the Virgin Mary that they not only clung to their faith, despite the appalling persecution of the local Catholic clergy, but also 'infected' a vast crowd of spectators on the last occasion that Mary appeared. Scores of people claimed to have seen the sun falling from the sky and rushing terrifyingly towards the earth. Science has names for these experiences which Paul lacked: epilepsy, schizophrenia, hysteria, mass hallucination. On another level, most of us have a minor 'vision' when we fall in love and suddenly another human being becomes endowed with extraordinary beauty and significance that transcend facts and reason, Paul's vision of the risen Jesus amounted to a lifelong love affair. He shared the visionary's absolute faith. From that moment, Jesus was no longer a subversive rebel who had deserved his death. He was alive and suffering in his followers on earth. Paul was literally blinded by his vision, and metaphorically he was blind to any objections based on mere reason, and certain of its final authority.

Today we are sceptical about visions; surely people shouldn't make lifelong decisions based on moments of abnormal excitement? The Church itself is notoriously hostile to visions, not surprisingly, because the visionary bypasses the authoritarian channels that God is supposed to use when he wants to get in touch with us. To explain away the supernatural nature of Paul's conversion it has been suggested that he had epilepsy. He writes to the Galatians about an illness: 'You never showed the least sign of being revolted or disgusted by my disease which was such a trial to you' (4: 14). This could be epilepsy or any unsightly illness. However, even if he had some kind of neurological or psychological illness that produced visions as frequently as Luke suggests in Acts of the Apostles that does not necessarily devalue them. God might just as easily use an illness or a disorder in the temporal lobe of the brain as use other natural phenomena. Many of the saints have had transcendental experiences that can now be seen as classic symptoms of recently discovered diseases. Joan of Arc's voices which called her to save France and for which she died, are common symptoms of schizophrenia. Teresa of Avila had a three-day vision of Hell which could well have been a severe epileptic attack, particularly as it was accompanied by a powerful stench, which is typical of the *aura* that an epileptic experiences before and sometimes during an attack. Paul's visions, if there is a natural explanation, could well have had a neurological cause.

In many ways Paul did not have a visionary temperament. He may have been vehement and passionate, extreme and excitable in his obsessions, but he was not a visionary in the sense of being whimsical or vaguely ecstatic in his approach to life. On the contrary, he was a man of practical common sense and efficiency. He had visions all his life, but he was always extraordinarily rational about them. For Paul they were merely episodes to be quickly incorporated into a rational structure. But even so, his faith was based on vision, not on reason. Whatever the Church feels about visions today, Christianity has been radically affected by this vision of Paul's.

Luke tells us that after his conversion the Lord sent one Ananias to Paul to give him back his sight. Ananias, a member of the Damascus church, was understandably sceptical about Paul's conversion, but the Lord was insistent.

Paul, he says, is 'my chosen instrument to bring my name before the pagans and pagan kings and before the people of Israel' (Acts 9: 15). Ananias was persuaded, went to Paul and restored his sight to him. After his baptism, Luke says, Paul stayed and preached in Damascus, alongside the other disciples. Paul himself has a very different story.

Luke's is the only detailed account of the conversion we possess. We can trust his account in its essentials; at the heart of his narrative are two elements which are fundamental to Paul's faith: the identity of the suffering Christ with believers, and Paul's gentile mission. He has excellent theological reasons for his story of Ananias. Unlike the epileptic or the schizophrenic, the Christian visionary does not have visions for his own sake; if a visionary is given such a privilege it is for the sake of the Christian community as well as for his own edification. In Luke's account, when Ananias cures his blindness, Paul's spiritual vision also is seen to be dependent on the already established Church, and Paul spent some time with the Damascus disciples, consolidating his faith within the Christian community. Luke, always anxious to depict a united Church, has edited things here. Paul describes the events immediately following his revelation quite differently:

> Then God, who had specially *chosen* me while I was *still in my mother's womb*,[1] called me through his grace and chose to reveal his Son in me, so that I might preach the Good News among the Pagans. I did not stop to discuss this with any human being, nor did I go up to Jerusalem to see those who were already apostles before me, but I went off to Arabia at once and later went straight back from there to Damascus.
>
> (Galatians 1: 15-17)

Instead of consolidating his faith with the apostles, it is 'three years' before Paul made any move to contact the Judaean church. (Galatians 1: 18). Like Luke, he is insistent

1. Isaiah 49: 1 and Jeremiah 1: 5.

that his vision was not just for himself; Christ called him because of his mission to the pagans. From the very first moment of his Christian life Paul went his own way and stridently insisted on his independence.

This may seem surprising; any new Christian today would surely relish the chance of meeting those apostles who had known Jesus when he was alive, but this does not seem to have interested Paul. Furthermore, there is no sense of Paul's considering himself inferior to the first apostles of Jesus – his vision of Jesus gave him an authority he thought equal to theirs:

> I taught you what I have been taught myself, namely that Christ died for our sins, in accordance with the Scriptures; that he appeared first to Cephas and secondly to the Twelve. Next he appeared to more than five hundred of the brethren at once, most of whom are still alive, though some may have died; and then he appeared to James, and then to all the apostles; and last of all he appeared to me too; it was as though I was born when no one was expecting it.
>
> I am the least of the apostles; in fact, since I persecuted the Church of God I hardly deserve the name of apostle, but by God's grace that is what I am, and the grace that he gave me has not been fruitless. On the contrary, I, or rather the grace of God that is in me, have worked harder than any of the others.

(1 Corinthians 15: 3-11)

What gave Paul full authority to teach as an apostle on an equal footing with Peter and James was his vision of Jesus. It was not a matter of going back to the historical sources and witnesses of Jesus' life on earth. To be an apostle, one who had a mission from Jesus to preach the good news of his resurrection, was not a matter of study and rational inquiry about Jesus' teaching and the authenticity of his claims. One had to have 'seen the Lord' as risen (1 Corinthians 9: 1). It is interesting to notice that Paul makes no distinction between his own vision of Jesus and those apparitions to Peter and the others. Where the gospels show Jesus as physically and incontrovertibly present to the apostles, able to eat and drink and be touched, Paul, who was writing much earlier, shows the events as entirely similar to his own violent vision, which he compares to an abnormal childbirth. The apparitions to Peter and James and the rest were probably visions like Paul's on the road to Damascus, rather than physical manifestations of the risen Lord. Paul does not suggest that they were any different, and the gospel story of the apparition on the road to Emmaus suggests a more Pauline vision than the other resurrection stories. The two disciples talk with Jesus for hours before recognising him, and at the moment of recognition Jesus disappears. Early Christian experience was not based on the rational but on irrational vision, and that gave the apostles authority to teach. Paul's vision in mode was the same as Peter's.

Why did Paul go to Arabia and stay away from the apostles for three years? Later he was anxious to forge a link with the Jerusalem church, yet it was to be three years before he made his first tentative approach. Paul was not deliberately avoiding the apostles. He did not feel they had much to teach him, true, but he would try all his missionary life to keep on good terms with them, with little real success. However, if he had gone to Peter and James directly after his vision on the Damascus road it is most unlikely that they would have taken him seriously. How could they trust him? He had left Jerusalem on a mission of persecution, after all. Luke preserves in Ananias' dismayed words, when he is told to baptise Paul, what would have been the quite understandable reaction to approaching Paul in any friendly spirit:

> Lord, several people have told me about this man and all the harm he has done to your saints in Jerusalem. He has only

come here because he holds a warrant from the chief priests
to arrest everybody who invokes your name.

(Acts 9: 13-15)

When Paul eventually approached the Jerusalem church he
was not, even three years after his conversion, welcomed
very warmly. If he had gone to them immediately his
reception would probably have been chillier still.

At the southernmost point of Biblical Judaea, at
Beersheba, the deserts of the Negev and Saudi Arabia begin.
It is probably this area that Paul means when he says that he
went to 'Arabia' immediately after his conversion. Why did
he choose this place, instead of returning home to Tarsus,
for example, or remaining quietly in Judaea? Apart from
Paul's bald statement we have no information about these
three years after Damascus; however, it is likely that the
desert gave Paul the chance to disappear for a while. Later,
when he presented himself to the churches, he could at least
show that he had acted seriously, that his faith was going to
last and that he had undergone in the desert the period of
purification traditional for Jews in Judaea. John the Baptist
had done it, so had Elijah the prophet, and there would be a
tradition that Jesus himself had started his mission by a
period of retreat in the desert, though Paul himself would
not have known about that. In the desert too Paul could
think over the implications of his vision, and doubtless here
he began to develop his theology.

It is a mistake to consider Paul living in the desert as a
kind of monk, contemplating for three years. There are two
facts crucial to Paul's belief that would have made this
impossible. The first is that Paul believed strongly that he
had been called to spread the gospel, the good news, about
Jesus to the pagans. This belief is essential to Paul's faith.
Christ called him not for himself, but 'so that I might preach
the good news about him to the Pagans' (Galatians 1: 16).

Whenever he talks of his conversion he mentions his mission; for him the two are inextricably combined. So it would be unlikely that with the conversion fresh in his experience he would wander off into the desert for three years and do nothing about his mission. The desert was not deserted; then, as now, the nomad bedouin travelled with their flocks from one waterhole to another. Their desert hospitality was and still is legendary, and Paul would have been dependent on their good offices. Later in his missionary travels he would also have lived rough, and as hitherto he seems to have led a bookish, urban life, it is possibly among the bedouin that he learned basic outdoor skills. But beside the bedouin, caravans of Nabatean traders, whose routes linked the Red Sea with the Mediterranean, also crossed the desert, which was punctuated by their great cities. Petra, Amira and Shivta are now only ruins, but in Paul's time they were large, populated cities. Petra, the 'rose-red' city, was one of the wonders of the ancient world. As well as proving his faith to the Judaean churches, therefore, the desert also gave Paul a chance to begin his mission to the gentiles.

There is a second reason why Paul would have wanted to begin his mission immediately: he hadn't got much time. Fundamental to Paul's faith is his firm belief that Jesus would shortly return in glory. This, we have seen, the first followers of Jesus believed implicitly. It was basic to early Christian faith. Jesus had risen from the dead, and Peter and his followers believed he would return in glory in their lifetime to establish the kingdom of God in Jerusalem. Paul's theology cannot be understood correctly without taking this into account. He referred to it as the *parousia* (the 'presence') of Christ. It runs as a persistent and integral theme through his letters:

> Brothers, this is what I mean: our time is growing short. Those who have wives should live as though they had none, and those who mourn should live as though they had

> nothing to mourn for; those who are enjoying life should live
> as though they had nothing to laugh about; those whose life
> is buying things should live as though they had nothing of
> their own; and those who have to deal with the world should
> not become engrossed in it. I say this because the world as we
> know it is passing away.
>
> (1 Corinthians: 7: 29-31)

Paul believed that he had a mission to preach the gospel to
the 'ends of the earth' and then, once everybody had had a
chance of salvation, Christ would return, having waited
only for the completion of Paul's work. Paul, believing that
he would see the *parousia* in his own lifetime, naturally
wished to start his mission immediately.

What was it that Paul was preaching to these pagans in the
desert? Why should the Nabateans or the bedouin be
interested in the coming of the Jewish Messiah, who would
shortly return to lead gentiles like themselves in chains?
One of the reasons why we have no record of these three
years in Paul's life is probably because his mission was
unsuccessful; consequently when Luke came to write his
account there were no Pauline churches in the area and no
traditions about him. Christianity has never taken root in
the Arab world. It is one of those cultures, like the Chinese
or Japanese, in which Christianity seems unable to flourish.
It was not until Paul took the gospel to his own Greco-
Roman world that he became successful; it was there – not
in Christ's Judaea – that Christianity survived.

At this point we realise that something happened to belief
in Jesus after Paul was converted on the road to Damascus,
because, as we know from the Epistles, Paul did not preach
about a Jewish Messiah. His vision had revealed to him that
whatever Christ had believed and done during his earthly
life, his resurrection had transformed him into something
completely different. Of course Paul, the Jew, believed that
Jesus was the Messiah. The name Krystos, 'the anointed
one', is a Greek translation of 'Messiah', but Paul believed

that Jesus had transformed the role of Messiah. Instead of dying a martyr for the Jewish nation and returning in triumph for the Jews alone, Paul believed that Christ had died as a sacrifice to God to save *all* men from sin.

The absolute nature of Paul's faith in his vision is extraordinary. He probably knew more about Jesus than any Christian alive today; he probably understood perfectly the essentially Jewish nature of Christ's mission. Earlier he had felt it his duty to persecute Jesus' followers, because of his loyalty to his race. He probably knew in far more detail the true story of Jesus' death because he did not have to rely, as we do, on the garbled accounts in the gospels. But for Paul these facts about the earthly Jesus were unimportant: 'If we did know Jesus according to the flesh, that is not how we know about him any longer' (2 Corinthians 5: 16). He had seen the risen Jesus and that vision had transformed the earthly Jesus into something quite different. When God raised Jesus from the dead he lifted him to a special relationship with himself and with the world. Paul's vision plunged him away from facts and logic into a new life in the desert and later as a migrant missionary that was entirely alien to everything he had ever known before.

In the concept of Christ dying to save all men from sin we can recognise the Christianity we know, and it seems that this concept was Paul's. It is true that in his summary of the faith in the resurrection which he repeats to the Corinthians he maintains that he has taught them only 'what I had been taught myself' (1 Corinthians 15: 3). Paul is always insistent that he learned his gospel directly from the Lord and not from men, so it is probable that he is not referring to the apostles here. Christ had taught him. It is probably true, however, that the apostles had incorporated some such notion into their early teaching. They were preaching a crucified Messiah, a difficult concept. Potential converts, hearing that Jesus had died by the scandalous death of crucifixion, would perhaps want to know why; hence some such notion as 'for our sins' was developed.

Exactly what that preposition 'for' meant for them we shall probably never know. Much scholarly ink has been spilt on the subject: did the apostles believe that Jesus died because of the sins of Israel; vicariously in the place of Israel; as a sacrifice to Yahweh on Israel's behalf? For the apostles, the cross was probably not as central as it was for Paul. For them it was a transitory phase that Jesus had gone through on his way to glory. From what we can tell from Acts, the early Church probably passed over the Crucifixion, being far more interested in the outpouring of the spirit that Jesus' resurrection had released, by heralding the last days of the messianic era. Like Paul, they were wholly centred on the idea of the *parousia*. Paul, however, preached only about Jesus crucified. It was he who developed most fully the notion of Jesus' sacrificial death. Most important was the idea that Christ's sacrifice had not been for Israel alone, but for mankind, an idea that the Jewish Christians would not have welcomed.

Once Christ is seen as dying for all men, then the phrase 'for our sins' takes on a deeper meaning, as it does in Paul. Human sacrifice was common in the ancient world, particularly when a new race or a new city was founded, and Judaism had a whole theology of sacrifice. Genesis tells the story of Abraham being commanded by God to sacrifice his son Isaac. Abraham, though he dearly loved Isaac, and Isaac was his only son, prepared to obey God and led Isaac to Mount Moriah, laid him down and drew the knife. At that moment the 'angel of the Lord' forbade Abraham to go any further. It had been only a test of Abraham's faith and he had passed the test triumphantly, proving himself worthy of Yahweh's regard. God did not require human sacrifice of his new nation; instead Abraham sacrificed a goat found nearby. The Temple was built on the site of Abraham's aborted sacrifice of Isaac and the Muslim mosque, the Dome of the Rock, which occupies the site of the old Temple, preserves the place. At the Temple only animal sacrifice was performed, for transgressions against the Law or as thank-offerings.

Sacrifice was the principal way, together with a solemn celebration of the feast of Atonement, for the Jews to approach God in contrition. A mechanical offering of a sacrifice could not atone, but the Jew was confident that as long as his heart was directed to God in sincere repentance, God was always ready to forgive his sins against the Law. Christians usually assume that the Jews of Jesus' time were crippled with guilt (when they were not bursting with complacency) about the impossible demands of the Law of Moses. Furthermore, it is believed that the Old Testament God is a God of wrath, and that it was Jesus who revealed God as a loving Father. But this idea is dispelled by even a cursory reading of the Old Testament, which is full of Yahweh's tenderness to Israel, and we have already seen that Jesus' teaching about a loving God was well within the traditions of rabbinic Judaism of the time. Instead of being crippled by guilt, the Jews had a more manageable concept of sin than the Christians have. Rabbi Samuel ben Nahman taught that on the day of creation when, instead of saying 'it is good', God said 'it is very good', he had created the 'evil impulse' to sin:

> *And behold it was very good.* This is the evil impulse. Is the evil impulse good? Yet were it not for the evil impulse no man would build a home, nor marry a wife, nor beget children, nor engage in trade. Solomon said, 'All labour and all excelling in work is a man's rivalry with his neighbour.'
>
> (Genesis Rabbah Ecclesiastes 4: 4)

In Judaism sin is a regrettable fact of life, but it should not fill the heart of man with despair. Everybody sins, but God will forgive. Moreover, the rabbi teaches that man would be the poorer without sin: the 'evil impulse' is also the source of much that is good and creative in man. That is why God

said his creation was 'very good'; on that day man became
fully human.

Paul has a much more frightening view of sin. For him sin
is not, as it would later become in Christian terminology, a
moral defect or an immoral act. It is a power, a power that
renders man helpless. Unredeemed man is a 'slave of sin', a
phrase that recurs constantly in Paul's letters. Thus
enslaved, man is helpless and impotent for good; even the
Law could not alter this. But now that Jesus has died on the
cross as a sacrifice for all men, all men can be saved:

> We wish you grace and peace of God our Father and of the
> Lord Jesus Christ, who in order to rescue us from this
> wicked world sacrificed himself for our sins, in accordance
> with the will of God our Father to whom be glory for ever.

(Galatians 1: 1-3)

Paul did not start out with a depressing sense of man
enslaved by the 'wicked world'. His vision had shown him
that *because* Christ died for all men, *therefore* all men had
been formerly enslaved by sin and needed redemption. If all
men sinned in Adam, far more important was the fact that all
men had been saved in Christ:

> If it is certain that through one man's fall so many died, it is
> even more certain that divine grace, coming through one
> man, Jesus Christ, came to so many as an abundant free gift.
> The results of the gift also outweigh the results of one man's
> sin: for after one single fall came judgement with a verdict of
> condemnation, now after many falls comes grace with its
> verdict of acquittal.

(Romans 5: 15-17)

If Paul's theology is essentially positive, this is not always
how he has been understood by later Christians. What we
have here is the embryonic doctrine of original sin, a sin
inherited from Adam and which must be removed by
baptism when a man enters the saving death of Christ, dies

with him to his sins and is freed from sin's slavery. This was an entirely new concept. Judaism had certainly believed that Adam's sin had involved his descendants, but the rabbis were not entirely sure how Adam's sin affected all men, apart from the fact that he became mortal. Judaism was too anxious to preserve human freedom and individual responsibility to regard the relation between Adam's sin and the sins of his descendants as causal. It did not hold that Adam's sin meant that he handed on to his descendants a vitiated nature, impotent for good, groaning under sin's slavery. Writing about man's natural unredeemed state, Paul has expressed himself memorably, and stamped on generations of Christians a sense of guilt about their 'natural' or 'unspiritual' selves:

> The fact is, I know of nothing good living in me – living that is in my unspiritual self – for though the will to do what is good is in me, the performance is not, with the result that instead of doing the good things I want to do, I carry out the sinful things I do not want. When I act against my will, then it is not my true self doing it, but sin which lives in me.

(Romans 7: 18-20)

For Paul the picture is a hopeful one, now he has been rescued from this impotent state by the saving death of Christ. Not all Christians have been able to write so positively. 'The whole clay of humanity is condemned clay,' wrote Augustine (*The City of God* 21). There is often a lugubriousness about the way Christians have dwelt on their sinfulness. Paul's impassioned depiction of the hopeless impotence of unredeemed man started a habit of guilt, because his successors have not alway remembered, or even realised, that he is talking in Romans 7 about man *before* the saving death of Christ. Augustine here writes in the terms of Paul's original sin about the individual sins of the Christian:

> For the law of sin is the fierce force of habit by which the

mind is drawn and held even against its will and yet deservedly because it had fallen wilfully into the habit.

(*Confessions* 8: 5)

It is a commonplace how many forms of Christianity induce a crippling sense of guilt; we need only recall Joyce's hell fire sermon in the *Portrait of the Artist as a Young Man*. When making the spiritual exercises of St Ignatius Loyola the retreatant spends a week contemplating his sins, his helplessness and the 'four last things'. The concept of Hell, which is remarkably absent from the New Testament considering the capital preachers have made of it since, has terrorised entire generations of Christians. It leads many to believe that their 'natural' selves are bad and ever ready to lure them to eternal danger.

Paul's teaching on sin offers no solution to the problem of guilt. Though his intention was otherwise, his teaching on sin could be said to increase guilt. In baptism, Paul says, a Christian enters Christ's sacrificial death, goes into the tomb with Christ and at the *parousia* – or when the individual Christian dies, whichever comes first – he will share in Christ's resurrection:

> If in union with Christ we have imitated his death, we shall also imitate him in his resurrection. We must realise that our former selves have been crucified with him to destroy this sinful body and to free us from the slavery of sin. When a man dies, he has, of course, finished with sin.

(Romans 6: 5-7)

However, the sad fact of the matter is that, as all Christians know, baptism or no baptism, Christians have not finished with sin. Of the individual sins of the Christian Paul has nothing to say. He is aware that even after baptism a Christian goes on sinning; his letters are full of exhortation and cries of horror at the sins of his converts. But his answer is a little too simple. It is all very well to assert that once a man has died with Christ in baptism he has 'of course finished with sin'. Such an assumption can make a Christian feel even more poignantly his unworthiness.

It is also true, although again this is something Paul did not intend, that the concept of unredeemed man as not only unfortunate but wicked is a dangerous one. On this notion of original sin Christians have justified their Crusades and their persecutions of infidels and pagans. It justifies insensitive missionary methods that often make us wince; it justifies that hint of superiority that we so often detect in Christians when they approach their 'godless' brothers.

Paul had no time to foresee all this. For him the contradiction of man 'finished with sin' but still sinning was part of a period of crisis. Man was looking forward to the imminent *parousia* and would not have time to struggle with the problem of sin all his life. Nor would he have time to develop a schizophrenia, seeing a fundamental split between his 'natural' self and his redeemed self, between the demands of the 'natural' and the 'supernatural' order. Over a period of two thousand years Christians have had ample time for the contradictions of Paul's message to develop into intolerance and self-loathing.

After a period in Damascus, when he was ejected from the city by King Aretas of the Nabateans, Paul turned towards Jerusalem. Luke gives us no account of his meeting with the apostles and we have only a cryptic version by Paul himself:

> Even when after three years I went up to Jerusalem to visit Cephas and stayed with him for fifteen days, I did not see any of the apostles; I saw only James, the brother of the Lord, and I swear before God that what I have written is the literal truth.
>
> (Galatians 1:18-21)

Later in Galatians, Paul speaks frankly about his disagreement with Peter (Cephas) and James, so the fact that no argument is recorded here indicates that this meeting was amicable. Yet it was probably no resounding success either:

that Paul stayed only for fifteen days and did not meet any of the other apostles, indeed did not do so for years to come, suggests he was not exactly given red-carpet treatment. Peter and Paul must have looked at one another with a certain amount of bewilderment.

They had much in common. Both believed that Jesus was the long expected Messiah and that he had risen from the dead; both had had visions of the risen Lord. Both believed that he would shortly return in glorious cosmic triumph. While they were waiting for Christ they probably both broke bread and drank the wine of the new covenant in Jesus' blood. It seems too that baptism was for both Peter and Paul a way of entering into this new covenant; the early followers of Jesus took over a Jewish ritual here. Belief in Jesus meant for both Peter and Paul a duty to spread the gospel of his death and resurrection.

But to whom? This was the problem. For Peter and James the good news was only for the Jews. Jesus' death and resurrection had been for the Jewish nation, his triumph would be a triumph for Israel. In the kingdom of God, which Jesus the Messiah would establish, sin would of course be overcome, but the gentiles would come to Jerusalem bound and in chains. Salvation was not for them. To Paul, Christ had died for all men; because he had therefore cancelled the whole nationalistic thrust of the mission of Jesus, it was inevitable that the stress on Christ's sacrifice 'for our sins' should be increased. Christ died not to establish the kingdom of Israel, but to redeem all men from sin and death. In Paul, Christianity as we know it began.

The initial chilliness of Paul's reception by the Jerusalem church was only the beginning of a conflict which would soon split the early Church right down the middle.

3 The break with Jerusalem

After his meeting with James and Peter, Paul went to Syria and Cilicia. There follows a period of about fifteen to seventeen years when we know practically nothing about Paul's movements. It is a substantial period of time – about three times as long as the period in the 50s when Paul was writing all his Epistles. All Paul says was that his preaching, which had hitherto been unsuccessful in Arabia, began to succeed so well that the news of it reached the churches in Judaea, 'and they gave glory to God for me' (Galatians 1:24).

Luke fills in the time for us, though it is uncertain how far we can rely on his account. Certainly Paul worked at Antioch, but Luke also tells us that Paul went on his first missionary journey at this time. Paul never mentions this journey. Some scholars have suggested that it happened considerably later, but in the absence of any real evidence to the contrary it is difficult to challenge Luke's chronology.

If Paul was chilled by his first encounter with Peter and James, there was no question yet of an open breach. Like a true Pharisee, James may well have said that he would 'wait and see' what happened to this surprising and embarrassing convert, and it seems that for these fifteen years Paul was working alongside the Jerusalem church. Antioch was a church founded by the Hellenistic Jews who fled Judea during the persecution following Stephen's death. Luke tells us that they continued to preach only to the Jews, but that 'some of them, who came from Cyprus and Cyrene, went to

Antioch where they started to preach to the Greeks, pro-claiming the Good News of the Lord Jesus to them as well' (Acts 11:20). Hearing about this, the Jerusalem church sent Barnabas to investigate, and, as it was a situation right after Paul's heart, Barnabas fetched Paul from Tarsus to Antioch, marking the start of a long companionship which seems to have ended in bitterness and conflict. Interestingly, after the arrival of Paul, the followers of Jesus in Antioch started to be called Christians for the first time. 'It was at Antioch that the disciples were first called "Christians" ' (Acts 11: 26) – probably a derisive nickname, as the pagans heard them preaching constantly about the Christ and using his name again and again.

It was Barnabas who accompanied Paul on his first missionary journey, Luke tells us, which took in Cyprus, Syria and Asia Minor. That Barnabas went along too sug-gests that James, the head of the Jerusalem church, was backing the new venture; and the fact that Paul and Bar-nabas always preached first in the synagogues may mean that it was conceived as a missionary journey to the diaspora Jews to tell them that the long-awaited Messiah had come. However, Paul's universal ideas meant that he turned to the gentiles, especially as the Jews often rejected the gospel. The success of Paul's preaching among the gentiles led ultimately to the surfacing of irreconcilable differences between Paul and Jerusalem.

Why was it that Paul, who was unsuccessful in Arabia, could now venture abroad with such lasting success? He was ideally placed to take the gospel into the Hellenistic world of the Roman Empire. Greek speaking and a Roman citizen, he belonged far more to the world of the empire than most Jews did, but also there were elements in Paul's gospel which would appeal strongly to the Greco-Roman world. Greek mythology, which the Romans had adopted, was full of figures who bore a fleeting resemblance to Jesus in Paul's story. Figures like Prometheus, who suffered for the sake of mankind, and Adonis, who died and rose again, meant that the story of Jesus was not entirely strange to Paul's converts. Admittedly, by this time nobody took the old Olympian religion seriously, but there was a strong spirit of religious quest in the empire during the first century. The decay of the old religion and the decline of ideals of the ancient world led to a disillusion and dissatisfaction not dissimilar to those felt in our own day, which leads many people to seek new religious answers. Some of the Greeks, we have seen, found their religious answer in Judaism, which was then a highly respected and attractive religion, with its strong moral sense, inspiring scriptures and impressive sense of history.

Other Greeks found an answer in the new mystery cults which were growing up at this time. The old Olympian religion was beginning to blend, in the syncretic habit of the Greek world, with Persian or Egyptian forms of worship. The cult of Dionysus, for instance, merged with that of Isis and Osiris. Because these cults were 'mysteries' their initiates were sworn to secrecy, and we have little idea what went on; most of our sources are late and unreliable. One common factor was the belief that the initiate died mystically with the dying god, to rise again with him in a series of weird and wonderful experiences. There were, as we shall see, important differences between Paul's gospel and these mysteries. The old idea that Paul was simply concocting a new mystery religion in Christianity is no longer seriously entertained. But Paul's preaching about a man who had died and risen again would have struck some chord in his pagan listeners. The idea of dying with Jesus in baptism and being released into a new freedom from sin's slavery would again be familiar.

Inevitably, Paul's audiences received his gospel according to their own preconceptions and, unconsciously perhaps, altered it subtly to fit in with their religious needs and habits. Inevitably too Paul would adapt his gospel slightly to meet the needs of his converts and help them understand, translating the Jewish Jesus into a Greek idiom. Even the Epistles, which were written so closely together that it is misleading to speak of a development, show something of the process of transformation. In what is generally accepted as his first Epistle, to the Thessalonians, Paul speaks of the *parousia* in terms of Judaism, using the Jewish apocalyptic imagery of angels and trumpets. A few years later, in his first Epistle to the Corinthians, Paul has adopted more of a Greek tone, in terms of body and soul. He uses Greek concepts like 'mystery' and 'gnosis', knowing that they will speak clearly to his converts.

Although Paul was translating the Jewish Jesus into an idiom that could be readily understood by the Greeks, even though he was now turning more and more to the gentiles, as the Jews rejected his message, there was never any question of Paul's rejecting Judaism itself. It is true that he believed that the old covenant with Israel had now been abrogated by Jesus' death – an idea which would have immense repercussions. However, he wanted to preserve the link with Judaism for a reason that separates his gospel sharply from the mystery cults, and that perhaps accounts for its success and endurance long after the demise of those cults. The mystery cults were based on half-forgotten myths and legends of vegetation and the natural world. Because the cults had no clear basis in reality, people often belonged to several. For Paul, Christianity was no mere myth; Jesus was a figure of very recent history. His death was not a beautiful legend like the story of Adonis; it had actually happened at a particular time and place. People could not be baptised into Jesus' death, which had actually happened, and join the cult of Dionysus at the same time, as though they were both possessed of the same reality. Christianity, Paul insisted, was historically true and had to be accepted as such.

Paul's vision of Jesus was not based on anything strictly rational that could be proven and argued like the tenets of

Greek philosophy, but the fact that Jesus had really lived and died was beyond question. Jesus' resurrection had transformed the material Jesus, but the historical reality of his life and death remained. The historical Jesus was a Jew and had come to Israel as its long-awaited Messiah. Through Judaism, through Jesus, God had save the world. This was no half-remembered myth.

Even though, increasingly and inevitably, Judaism firmly rejected Paul and his message, Paul never rejected Judaism, unlike the evangelists Matthew and John. His separation from Judaism was a great grief to him:

> What I want to say is this: my sorrow is so great, my mental anguish so endless, I would willingly be condemned and be cut off from Christ if it could help my brothers in Israel, my own flesh and blood. They were adopted as sons, they were given the glory and the covenants; the Law and the ritual were drawn up for them and the promises were made for them. They are descended from the patriachs and from their flesh and blood came Christ who is above all, God for ever blessed! Amen.

(Romans 9: 2-5)

Paul's roots as well as Jesus' were in Judaism. Through Judaism, God's plan for mankind could be traced historically back to the dawn of mankind. What distinguished the Jewish scriptures was that they embraced the history of mankind from the first moment of creation; through Judaism, Christianity was history's triumphant conclusion. Through Moses and Abraham, God had shaped the later history of his people, but even before Abraham, his plan could be seen through Adam, the covenant with men in the very act of creation itself. Paul also used Jewish history to argue his points and to show how Christ was 'above all', seeing Adam as a type, or rather antitype, of Jesus; seeing Abraham as the father, through Christ, of all believers now, not just of the Jews; seeing Moses and his Law as having a transitional role while mankind was waiting for the fullness of God's revelation in Christ. Far from intending to cut Christianity off from Judaism, Paul insisted that Christians were the 'true Israel'. Through the history of Judaism, Christianity could remain firmly in the world of actuality and not degenerate into fiction. The irrational nature of Paul's own vision must have made him cling all the more strongly to the historical aspects of his faith.

Luke's colourful account of Paul's missionary journey smacks of myth rather than of history. Nevertheless there are two incidents which deserve discussion, because they express something of the hopes and problems that Paul would have encountered in the pagan world.

On Cyprus, Luke says, the Roman governor Sergius Paulus was converted to Christianity. The story is an example of the cruder aspects of Luke's narrative. Sergius Paulus is stunned into faith, because of the way Paul blinds his rival, the magician Bar-Jesus or Elymas Magos, who was trying to prevent the governor's conversion:

> 'You utter fraud, you impostor, you son of the devil, you enemy of all true religion, why don't you stop twisting the straightforward ways of the Lord. Now watch how the hand of the Lord will strike you; you will be blind and for a time you will not see the sun.' That instant everything went misty and dark for him, and he groped about to find someone to lead him by the hand.
>
> (Acts 13: 10-11)

This dubious method of converting Sergius Paulus should not be allowed to obscure the possible significance of the story for Paul. Paul had little time for the pagan world. He speaks with disgust of 'their filthy enjoyments and degrading pleasures' (Romans 1: 24). But he was an admirer of Rome. This is one of the things that divides him most strongly from the Judaean Jews, who for the most part were so hostile to the empire that they eventually perished in a revolt against it. Far from wishing to rebel, Paul continually urged the duty of civil obedience:

> You must obey all the governing authorities. Since all government comes from God, the civil authorities were appointed by God, and so anyone who resists authority is rebelling against God's decision, and such an act is bound to be punished. Good behaviour is not afraid of magistrates; only criminals have anything to fear. If you want to live without being afraid of authority, you must live honestly and authority may even honour you. The state is there to serve God for your benefit. If you break the law, however, you may well have fear: the bearing of the sword has its significance. The authorities are there to serve God: they carry out God's revenge by punishing wrongdoers. You must obey, therefore, not only because you are afraid of being punished, but also for conscience's sake. This is also the reason why you must pay taxes, since all government officials are God's officers. They serve God by collecting taxes. Pay every government official what he has a right to ask – whether it be direct tax or indirect, fear or honour.
>
> (Romans 13:1-7)

The difference between Paul's and Jesus' attitude to tax collectors marks the way Paul began to translate the Judaean Jesus for the Roman world. Paul's respect for the empire made him urge not merely cooperation but positive support. We shall see that he wanted to use the empire to further the gospel; thus the conversion of Sergius Paulus, a figure of the Roman establishment and Paul's first important Roman convert, would have been most significant for him. But it is also true that the conversion may well mark the first moment of Christianity's ultimate corruption, as Paul's mystical faith seeks entanglement with a political ruling class.

The other incident to be discussed occurred at Lystra. Paul had healed a cripple. Far from leading the astonished Lycaonians to instant faith in Jesus, the event confirmed them in their paganism:

When the crowd saw what Paul had done they shouted . . . 'These people are gods who have come down to us disguised as men.' They addressed Barnabas as Zeus, and since Paul was the principal speaker they called him Hermes. The priests of Zeus-outside-the-Gate, proposing that all the people should offer sacrifice with them, brought garlanded oxen to the gates. When the apostles Barnabas and Paul heard what was happening they tore their clothes and rushed into the crowd, shouting, 'Friends, what do you think you are doing? We are only human beings like you. We have come with good news to make you turn from these empty idols to the living God who made heaven and earth and the sea and all that these hold. In the past he allowed each nation to go its own way; but even then he did not leave you without evidence of himself in the good things he does for you: he sends you rain from heaven, he makes your crops grow when they should, he gives you food and makes you happy.' Even this speech, however, was scarcely enough to stop the crowd offering them sacrifice.

(Acts 14: 11-18)

It is a good story, vividly told; the consternation of the two strict monotheists, Paul and Barnabas, comes through the narrative as they attempt to grapple with a situation they could scarcely have been able to imagine. Here was a religious world which was vastly different from Judaism: here we see paganism responding to Paul's message in its own terms, and only just being restrained from interpreting the gospel blasphemously. This kind of confrontation with paganism during his missionary journeys would have been incomprehensible to the Jerusalem church. In orthodox Jews like James it may have increased a distrust of the stubborn habits of idolatry among the gentiles whom Judaism, for fear of contamination, had shunned. Paul's new gentile converts in Cyprus and Asia Minor belonged to this world; in them too undesirable habits stubbornly clung on, even after their conversion. What was to be the relationship between these gentile converts and the Jewish church in Jerusalem? How were they to coexist in the new religion?

It was this problem which Paul set himself to solve when he returned to Antioch in AD 50. In Acts, Luke says that some 'men came down from Judaea and taught the brothers "Unless you have yourselves circumcised in the tradition of Moses you cannot be saved" ' (Acts 15:1). This, he explains, caused disagreement and led ultimately to Paul and Barnabas going up to Jerusalem to discuss the matter with the apostles there.

The hardliners from Judaea, who included a number of Pharisees, were insistent on the predominantly Jewish nature of the new faith. There might well be a new covenant in Jesus' blood; they might well differ from some of their fellow Jews about Jesus being the Messiah, but they were still staunch members of the chosen people. Had they been able to separate these two inextricable elements, they might have said they were Jews first and followers of Jesus second. That Paul was bringing gentiles into the Church in such large numbers could not have delighted them. They considered themselves a Jewish sect, holy to Yahweh.

The Jewish concept of holiness is quite different from the later Christian concept of a high degree of virtue and goodness. For the Jew, to be holy meant to be separate: God dwelt with them. In Jerusalem, the holy city, he dwelt in the Temple, in the holy of holies, where nobody except the high priest was allowed to enter. In order to live up to this privilege Israel had to separate herself from all the contaminating influences of the pagan world. She had to live in purity, apart from gentile idolatry and immorality. While the Israelites were living in the desert, after the escape from Egypt, because Yahweh dwelt in the camp with them, the camp had to be kept pure and undefiled:

> Order the sons of Israel to put out of the camp all lepers, and all who suffer from a discharge, or who have become unclean

by touching a corpse. Man or woman, you must not defile in
this way the camp where I dwell among them.

(Numbers 5: 2-3)

Later, when they were settled in the Holy Land, they had to
beware of subtler contamination, since the inhabitants and
neighbours of Canaan practised an attractive idolatry. Later
still, during exile in Babylon after the Jews were deported
from the Holy Land, the dangers of spiritual contamination
were still greater. 'Be ye Holy even as I am Holy,' Yahweh
had commanded them (Leviticus 19: 2). He dwelt separate
and apart in the Temple:

> Go away, go away, leave that place, touch nothing unclean,
>   Get out of her, purify yourselves, you who carry the
> vessels of Yahweh . . .

(Isaiah 52: 11)

Thus the prophet commands the chosen people during the
Babylonian captivity. This is why the Jews would not
contaminate themselves by entering the houses of the
Romans who lived in the Holy Land.

The arrival in the midst of the Nazarenes sect of a large
number of pagan converts caused the Jewish Christians
considerable alarm. Like the new Christians of Lystra, these
converted gentiles had yet to shed all their pagan habits.
How were Jewish Christians to guard against this contaminating presence? At a time when James and Peter were
preparing for the establishment of the kingdom of God, the
hardliners among the Pharisees, James' party, insisted that
to be received into the new sect the newcomers had to be
circumcised and accept the Law of Moses, the Torah.

To understand their position, we must look at the importance of these two elements in Judaism. When God called
Abraham and entered into a covenant with him, he made
Abraham, at the age of ninety-nine, circumcise himself, as
well as Ishmael, his son by the handmaiden Hagar, and all
the men of his household. God undertook to be Abraham's

God 'and the God of your descendants after you. I will give to you and to your descendants after you the land you are living in, the whole land of Canaan, to own in perpetuity, and I will be your God' (Genesis 17: 8). In return Abraham had to fulfil his side of the bargain:

> God said to Abraham, 'You on your part shall maintain my Covenant yourself and your descendants after you, generation after generation. Now this is my Covenant which you are to maintain between myself and you, and your descendants after you: all your males must be circumcised. You shall circumcise your foreskin, and this shall be the sign of the Covenant between myself and you. When they are eight days old all your male children must be circumcised, generation after generation of them, no matter whether they be born within the household or bought from a foreigner not one of your descendants. They must always be circumcised, both those born within the household and those who have been bought. My Covenant shall be marked on your bodies as a mark in perpetuity. The uncircumcised male, whose foreskin has not been circumcised, such a man shall be cut off from his people: he has violated my Covenant.
>
> (Genesis 17: 9-14)

It is an uncompromising demand. Those who are not circumcised cannot belong to the covenant. The gentile converts of Paul were 'foreigners'. If they wished to enter the Jewish sect of the Nazarenes, they had to accept circumcision, otherwise they were outside the covenant Yahweh had made with Israel.

The Law of Moses was as sacred to the Jews as circumcision. When God had led the Israelites out of Egypt under the leadership of Moses, he had revealed himself to Moses in the theophany on Mount Sinai. There too he had given them the Law, the Torah, to show his holy people how he wished them to live as members of his covenant. The Ten Commandments, inscribed by God on stone tablets, were the heart of the Torah, but over the centuries it had been developed into the elaborate legislation found in the Pentateuch, the first five books of the Old Testament. In the Torah the Israelites knew how God wished them to order their lives. It was an indispensable part of the covenant.

Christians whose only knowledge of Judaism comes from the New Testament are accustomed to regard the Law of Moses as extremely burdensome, a spiritual danger. The Jews of the time of Jesus and Paul, they believe from the evidence of the gospels and the Epistles, substituted minute observance for spiritual commitment. They believed that their observance of the Law and their 'good works' could save them, which induced spiritual pride and complacency. However, it must be remembered that the gospels were written by churches which by that time were having great problems with the Jews; hence their picture of the Torah is influenced by conflict and by ignorance of Palestinian Judaism before the destruction of Jerusalem in AD 70. The reality is quite different. Far from seeing the Torah as imposing an impossible burden on them, the Jews regarded it as a joy and a privilege:

> Meditating all day on your Law,
>   How I have come to love it!
> By your commandment, ever mine,
>   how much wiser you have made me than my enemies!
> How much subtler than my teachers,
>   through meditating on your decrees . . .
> Your decrees are so wonderful
>   my soul cannot but respect them.
> As your word unfolds, it gives light,
>   and the simple understand.
> I open my mouth, panting
>   eagerly for your commandments.
> Turn to me please, pity me,
>   as you should those who love your name.
> Direct my steps as you have promised,
>   let evil win no power over me.
> Rescue me from human oppression;

I will observe your precepts.
Treat your servant kindly,
    teach me your statutes.
My eyes stream with tears,
    because others disregard your Law.

(Psalm 119: 97-99, 129-36)

Here the Israelite longs to learn more about the Law; far from being complacent about his observance, he shows a childlike humility in his approach to God and prays for more guidance. Yet the New Testament implies that by the time of Jesus, this ideal had declined, replaced by a hard self-righteousness. Such attitudes, it is said, made Judaism reject Jesus.

By the time of Jesus, the two main Judaic interpretations of the Torah were represented by the two politico-religious parties, the Sadducees and the Pharisees. The Sadducees, the aristocratic priestly caste, were devoted to Temple worship and sacrifical ritual. Their veneration of the Law consisted in conservatism. They would not accept innovation, but insisted on preserving the letter of the Law as it was written in the Pentateuch. The Pharisees had a very different approach. They believed the Torah could be brought up to date and applied to the problems of contemporary life, private and public. Far from being the reactionary sect that appears in the gospels, they were by far the most flexible of the Jews of Jesus' day, innovators alive to new theological developments, such as the idea of the resurrection of the virtuous dead when the Messiah inaugurated the kingdom of God. Where the Sadducees were centred on Temple worship, the Pharisees were a power in the synagogues. After the Babylonian exile, when the captive Jews had been unable to sacrifice at the Temple of Solomon in Jerusalem, the synagogues had grown up as an important substitute. There the worship was confined to the reading and the explanation of the scriptures and to prayer – a system for which there is no parallel in the ancient history of religion.

In the synagogues they explored the full implications of the Law in a tradition of oral teaching. From the relative ease with which the Jews adapted to the loss of the Temple and the possibility of sacrifice when Jerusalem was destroyed in AD 70, it seems that Judaism was moving away from the idea of ritual animal sacrifice towards the synagogue system, the preserve of the Pharisees and scribal teachers. Today most rabbis are to all intents and purposes Pharisees, continuing the system of synagogue worship and Torah study.

It is not true, *pace* the gospels and Epistles, that any Jew of the time of Jesus thought he could be 'saved' and justified by minute observance of the Torah. For the Jew, the initiative in salvation had been taken by God; indeed, the Pharisees insisted that man could take no credit for his 'good works'. Rabbi Johanan says: 'If thou hast wrought much in the Law, claim not merit for thyself, for to this end wast thou created' (Aboth 2: 8). Jesus speaks in exactly the same spirit as the great rabbi: 'When you have done all that you are commanded to do say this: We are unprofitable servants, we have only done what was our duty' (Luke 17: 7). The Pharisaic study of the Law is usually presented as something arid and souless, but for the Pharisees it was a means of coming close to God, not performed solitarily with dusty tomes in libraries, but conducted by means of debate and by prayer, as a community exercise. 'Where two or three speak of the Torah together, God [the *Shekinah*] is with them' (Aboth 3: 2).

The spirit of humility and joy that we noted in the Psalms, when the psalmist sings of the Law, was not abandoned by Judaism. To a stranger, the Law does seem complicated and obscure, but then our twentieth-century legal system, code of manners and customs would seem equally obscure to someone of another culture. Most of the Torah's commandments, the *mitzvot*, would have been fulfilled by a Jew as a matter of course. Rabbi Meir says: 'There is no man in Israel who does not fulfil a hundred *mitzvot* every day'

(Tosefta Berakoth 7: 24). The rabbis' discussions about the minute commandments and their implications were not meant to add a greater burden, but rather to lessen anxiety: when a man knew exactly what his duty was he did not have the worry of uncertainty; and far from being a cruel taskmaster, the God of the Pharisees was always ready to forgive his children.

The gospel parable of the Pharisee and the publican epitomises the distorted portrait of the Pharisee as one who is delighted with himself and who relies on his good works to please God:

> Jesus spoke the following parable to some people who prided themselves on being virtuous and despised everyone else. 'Two men went up to the Temple to pray, one a Pharisee and the other a tax collector. The Pharisee stood there and said this prayer to himself, "I thank you, God, that I am not grasping, unjust, adulterous like the rest of mankind, and particularly that I am not like this tax collector here. I fast twice a week – I pay tithes on all I get." The tax collector stood some distance away, not daring even to raise his eyes to heaven – but he beat his breast and said, "God, be merciful to me, a sinner." This man, I tell you, went home again at rights with God.'
>
> (Luke 18: 9-14)

Despite the gospel presentation of the Pharisees as sublimely confident of their virtue, measured in their external observance of the Torah, in the writings and prayers of the rabbis of the time of Jesus and later we find no such complacency. Nor is there any notion that the Law is a burden. The rabbis are clear that the election of Israel is a gift of God, a privilege not to be earned by good deeds; salvation is entirely on God's loving initiative. Like the psalmist, the rabbis see the Torah as a proof of God's special love of Israel: 'At Sinai He appeared to them as an old man, full of mercy' (Mekilta Bahodesh 5: 212, ii, 231; to 20.2). Again

Rabbi Hananiah ben Aksashya sees the multitude of commandments as demonstrating God's love and favour:

> The Holy One, Blessed is He, was minded to grant merit to Israel; therefore hath he multiplied for them the Law and the commandments, as it is written, 'It pleased the Lord for his righteousness' sake to magnify the Law and make it honourable.'

(Mishnah, Isaiah 42: 21)

The Jewish Christians in Judea wanted to remain within mainstream Judaism. Circumcision was vital, just as the Torah was indispensable. It was for Judaism that Jesus had died, and if gentile converts wanted to enter their sect, it was essential that they accept the Jewish ways. Only thus could they prepare for the kingdom of God inaugurated by Jesus' triumphant return.

Paul refused to accept this. He believed that Christ's sacrificial death had cancelled out the old covenant. It was not simply a matter of expediency. Obviously a gentile convert would think not twice but several times before undergoing circumcision, and the prospect of learning, as an outsider, the complications of the Torah and changing his way of life would have been daunting. So if James and his Pharisees had carried the day there would have been few pagan converts to Christianity. However, Paul was not thinking of convenience. He had been a committed Pharisee, 'faultless' in the Law, before his conversion. He had valued it and loved it. Now he saw that its day was over. Circumcision and the Torah had been means to salvation before the death of Jesus, but there was no longer any need for either. There was now only one way to salvation; participation in the death of Jesus. The Law had been superseded by the redemption brought about by Jesus:

> Before faith came, we were allowed no freedom by the Law; we were being looked after till faith was revealed. The Law was to be our guardian until Christ came and we could be

justified by faith. Now that time has come we are no longer under that guardian, and you are, all of you, sons of God through faith in Jesus Christ. All baptised in Christ, you have all clothed yourselves in Christ and there are no more distinctions between Jew and Greek, slave or free, male and female, but you are all one in Christ Jesus. Merely by belonging to Christ you are the posterity of Abraham, the heirs he was promised.

(Galatians 3: 23-29)

Paul's conversion had been far more radical than that of the apostles. It caused him to leave behind many of the things that had been most precious to him and rethink the idea of salvation. Simply by being baptised, the gentile convert was a son of Abraham, a member of the new Israel – something no strict Jewish Christian, proudly maintaining the 'holiness' of Israel, could ever accept. Paul firmly faced strong and dedicated opposition.

The Jewish Christians had perhaps envisaged making the occasional gentile convert. Luke, once again seeking to prove Church unity, tells the story of the Roman centurion Cornelius, to show Peter in agreement with Paul that gentiles were exempt from the Law if they were baptised. For years Cornelius had been a Godfearer, and an angel appeared to him to tell him that his long fidelity was to be rewarded. He was to go to Jaffa and present himself to Peter, who was lodging there at that time. While Cornelius was on the road from Caesarea to Jaffa, Peter was also having a vision. A sheet was let down from Heaven and when it reached the ground Peter saw that it contained 'all sorts of animals and wild beasts – everything possible that could walk, crawl or fly' (Acts 11: 6). A voice commanded Peter to eat these animals. Peter objected, as many of them were declared unclean by the Law. Three times the command was made and each time Peter refused. Eventually the voice said: 'What God has made clean, you have no right to call profane' (Acts 11: 10). When Cornelius arrived shortly afterwards, Peter understood the meaning of the vision: 'God does not have favourites but that anybody of any nationality who fears God and does what is right is acceptable to him' (Acts 10: 34-35). It is not for Peter to say any more that the gentiles are 'unclean'; indeed, when Cornelius was baptised he at once received the holy spirit, to confirm Peter's insight. The Jews who were present, who were worried about admitting an uncircumcised pagan into their midst, now saw that God would impart his spirit to the pagans as well as to themselves. They amicably agreed that God can 'evidently grant even the pagans the repentance that leads to life' (Acts 11: 18).

The account reads like a real incident, and it is probably true that a Roman centurion, Cornelius, a Godfearer who 'gave generously to Jewish causes' (Acts 10: 2), was permitted to enter the Church. Like the eunuch whom Philip baptised, these occasional conversions were acceptable to the Jewish Christians. However, when Paul started talking about preaching the gospel to the ends of the earth, insisting that Christ had died for *all* men and that the old covenant was over, this was too much. Devout Jewish believers in Jesus, waiting faithfully for his return, still insisted on scrupulous fidelity to Judaism as a preparation.

If the Cornelius story is based on truth, Luke's story of the placid acceptance of Pauline universality is more dubious. He was writing at the end of the first century, by which time Paul's views had become Church policy and Christians had been ejected from Judaism. Peter's remarks about Cornelius represent the popular, diluted Paulinism that was then generally accepted. The reality was different, and this account is one of Luke's most obvious occasions of whitewashing. He says that after the Pharisees came to Antioch to insist that the gentiles were circumcised and accept the Torah, Paul and Barnabas went up to Jerusalem as delegates of the church of Antioch. Then there was a council of all the apostles and elders, presided over by Peter and by

James, who overrode Peter and made the final decision. Paul and Barnabas were merely delegates from Antioch, subservient to the decrees of the council. There seems to have been no disagreement. Peter and James overruled the hardliner Pharisees, who were insisting on circumcision and the Law. 'It would only provoke God's anger now, surely,' Peter suggested, 'if you imposed on the disciples the very burden that neither we nor our ancestors were strong enough to support. Remember, we believe that we are saved in the same way as they are: through the grace of the Lord Jesus' (Acts 15: 10-11). This piece of Paulinism was successful in silencing the whole assembly, who then listened with admiration to Paul's and Barnabas' account of 'all the signs and wonders God had worked through them among the Pagans (Acts 15: 12). James then decided that, in order to facilitate pagan conversion, he would issue a decree freeing gentile converts from full Judaic practices:

> The apostles and elders, your brothers, send greetings to the brothers of pagan birth in Antioch, Syria and Cilicia. We hear that some of our members have disturbed you with their demands and have unsettled your minds. They acted without any authority from us, and so we have unanimously decided to elect delegates and to send them to you with Barnabas and Paul, men we respect highly who have dedicated their lives to the name of our Lord Jesus Christ. Accordingly we are sending you Judas and Silas, who will confirm by word of mouth what we have written in this letter. It has been decided by the Holy Spirit and by ourselves not to saddle you with any burden beyond these essentials; you are to abstain from food sacrificed to idols, from blood, from the meat of strangled animals and from fornication. Avoid these, and you will do what is right. Farewell.

(Acts 15: 23-29)

Alas, this amicable solution to the problem seems to have been an invention of Luke's.

Paul, writing in about AD 54, four or five years after the

event, was still seething with bitterness that this original meeting had caused. His converts in Galatia seemed to have been listening, much to Paul's horror, to Jewish Christians who still insisted on the necessity of circumcision and observance of the Torah. Paul wrote angrily to them, asserting his own authority and that of his gospel. In his account there does not seem to have been a full council of the Church at all, but a private meeting between himself, Barnabas, and Peter, James and John. He had taken the initiative about the meeting himself, he insisted: 'I went up as a result of a revelation' – perhaps one of his visions – 'and privately I laid before the leading men the Good News as I proclaim it among the Pagans' (Galatians 2: 2).

If Paul did have a vision, here is an example of how he used them to further a piece of effective policy. Paul and Barnabas brought with them Titus, one of the gentile converts, as a kind of visual aid to force the issue. Paul refused to have Titus circumcised and then presumably looked appraisingly at James and asked him what he intended to do about it. 'And what happened?' he wrote 'Even though Titus, who had come with me, is a Greek, he was not obliged to be circumcised' (Galatians 2: 3). Running under the narrative, even though Paul is writing here about a compromise, a victory for himself, is an insubordination towards the leaders of the Church that is very different from Luke's pious account of the deference with which the assembly listened to James and Peter. The suggestion of acrimony and rivalry is unmistakable:

> The question [of circumcision] had only come up, because some, who do not really belong to the brotherhood, have furtively crept in to spy on the liberty we enjoy in Christ Jesus, and want to reduce us all to slavery. I was so deter-mined to safeguard for you the true meaning of the Good News, that I refused even out of deference to yield to such people for one minute. As a result, these people who are acknowledged leaders – not that their importance matters to

me, since God has no favourites – these leaders, I say, had nothing to add to the Good News as I preach it.

(Galatians 2: 4-7).

There was a fight, but finally victory for Paul. His mission to the uncircumcised pagans was confirmed and put on a par with Peter's mission to the Jews. The 'pillars', as Paul insists on calling Peter, James and John, decided that Christ had inspired both missions. All they asked was that Paul should 'remember to help the poor' in Judaea and collect a gift of money from the gentile converts as an offering to the Jerusalem church. This, Paul says, he 'was anxious to do'.

So far, so good. By a careful and perhaps rebellious policy Paul had carried the day. To insist on the Law as an essential for salvation was to denigrate the power of the saving death of Jesus. Of that Paul was convinced, and persuading James and Peter to take this radical step was a triumph. Church unity had been preserved; so had the essence of Paul's gospel. Christianity had preserved its link with Judaism by maintaining its unity with the Jerusalem church. That this was important to Paul we can see from the fact that he felt it necessary to go and discuss the matter at all. It was not that he felt that the 'pillars' were superior to him or that he had to bow to their decision – his own conversion vision made him an apostle equal to them. Paul is not like a tear-away young bishop having to get permission from Peter the Pope. From the moment of his conversion Paul acted independently, relying on direct inspiration from Christ, not on the words of men. That Paul did not simply go off on his missionary journey shows that he wanted to keep on good terms with the Jerusalem church, a desire which lasted throughout his missionary life, even after the split had occurred.

The real trouble came later that year at Antioch, when first Peter and then friends of James came for a visit. It seems that at first Peter was happy to mingle and eat with the gentile converts, but later deferred to the stricter party of James:

When Cephas came to Antioch, however, I opposed him to his face, since he was manifestly in the wrong. His custom had been to eat with the pagans, but after certain friends of James arrived he stopped doing this and kept away from them altogether for fear of the group that insisted upon circumcision. The other Jews joined him in this pretence, and even Barnabas felt himself obliged to copy their behaviour.

(Galatians 2: 11-13).

This shows a rather different Peter from the determined figure of Luke's Cornelius story. Far from carrying the day on this matter, he is seen wavering weakly between the Pauline and the Jamesian parties. Instead of seeing that 'what God has made clean, you have no right to call profane', Peter withdrew from the gentile converts, who were not, of course, fulfilling the Jewish dietary laws. When Peter, one of the leading Christians, behaved like this, Paul had to object. This was reducing his converts to second-class status in the Church. If Peter felt contaminated by mingling with baptised gentile Christians then the agreement they had made earlier in the year meant nothing. For Paul it was fundamental that in Christ there were no divisions, no favourites, 'neither Jew nor Greek'. There was absolute equality, a 'new creation' (2 Corinthians 5: 17). Peter's withdrawal meant also that he was not taking baptism seriously. These converts had 'entered the tomb' (Romans 6: 4) with Christ when they were baptised, which meant that they had participated in Jesus' death and were fully saved. Circumcision and the Law were now irrelevant. If Peter thought otherwise he was 'an enemy at the cross of Christ' (Philippians 3: 18).

Paul spoke out:

When I saw they were not respecting the true meaning of the Good News, I said to Cephas in front of everyone: 'In spite of being a Jew, you live like the pagans and not like the Jews, so you have no right to make the pagans copy Jewish ways.'

(Galatians 2: 14)

Peter had been content to associate with the pagans before James' friends had appeared on the scene. He had been trying to 'have it both ways'. As Paul points out a little later: 'If the Law can justify us, there is no point in the death of Christ' (Galatians 2: 21). Christ's death had meant a radical new departure and Peter had denied this.

The dispute between Peter and Paul, and by implication between James' Pharisaic party and Paul, started a bitter conflict. There is no hint of Paul's public denunciation of Peter having been resolved. If it had, Paul would surely have used any compromise or climbing down on Peter's and James' part – something Paul never dreamt of doing where his gospel was concerned – as a trump card in his dispute with the Judaising Christians of Galatia. But he leaves the matter in his Epistle with his angry words, and then goes on to develop his own theological argument: 'Though we were born Jews and not Pagan sinners, we acknowledge that what makes a man righteous is not obedience to the Law, but faith in Jesus Christ' (Galatians 2: 15). That the dispute between Paul and the strict Jewish Christians was a bitter one emerges in the tone of the Epistle to the Galatians. Luke's attempts to paper over this wide crack in the early Church and depict unanimous acceptance of Paul's mission and gospel cannot be believed.

Luke's account in Acts shows some signs of the dispute. Immediately after the account of the council of Jerusalem, when Paul is about to set out on his second missionary journey, we read this sad passage:

On a later occasion Paul said to Barnabas, 'Let us go back and visit all the towns where we preached the word of the Lord, so that we can see how the brothers are doing.' Barnabas suggested taking John Mark, but Paul was not in favour of taking along the very man who had deserted them in Pamphylia and had refused to share in their work.

After a violent quarrel they parted company, and Barnabas sailed off with Mark to Cyprus. Before Paul left, he chose Silas to accompany him and was commended by the brothers to the grace of God.

(Acts 15: 36-40)

In the narrative (Acts 13: 3) there is no hint of any real rupture between Paul and John Mark, a Jewish Christian who lived in Judaea. Luke simply says, as usual hiding the suggestion of disagreement, that 'Paul and his friends went by sea from Paphos to Pamphylia where John left them to go back to Jerusalem.' But Luke's source later forbids him to deny that this was an occasion of real conflict. We know from Galatians that even Barnabas sided with Peter at Antioch and it would seem that this was part of the same dispute. Paul's companion of over twelve years parted company with him at this point over the issue of circumcision and the Law.

Paul was a passionate and uncompromising man. One moment he was on a mission of persecution against Jesus' disciples, the next, after his vision, he was one of the most ardent disciples of Jesus himself. It was all or nothing. For him Christ's death shattered the *status quo* and marked the end of everything that Jews valued and prized so highly. But Paul was also a clear and logical thinker. His vision cut impatiently through Peter's muddle-headedness at Antioch and polarised a problem which might otherwise never have come to a head. Jesus' first followers were all Jewish. Today Jesus' followers are not Jews. This radical departure is due to Paul.

It is likely that were it not for Paul, Christianity would have remained a Jewish sect. He effected a schism in the early Church. Most of the Nazarenes would have been wiped out in AD 70 when Jerusalem was destroyed by the Romans. In the third century we can still read about Jewish Christians. In Capernaum, for example, they worshipped at the site of the house where Peter lived when he was a poor fisherman before Christ called him. These Jewish Christians were known eventually by their fellow Jews as the *minim*, the heretics, and you cannot be a heretic unless you still maintain that you are within the fold. Eventually even these followers fell back into Judaism, as was inevitable when Christ failed to reappear. For Jewish Christians the failure of the *parousia* was a death blow. After AD 70 the Holy Land was no more; Jerusalem was destroyed and the Temple was in ruins. How could Jesus return to establish the kingdom of God in Jerusalem? And where had Jesus been, what had he been doing to allow his people to be defeated by the Romans? Gentile Christians in the Pauline churches had a real problem too about the *parousia*, but differently focused. The destruction of Jerusalem was by no means the end of their hopes. Even though they went on hoping and expected the *parousia* imminently, by the end of the first century traditions about a mystical kingdom in the hearts of men are creeping into gospel writings.

The gospel stories still present the parables of Jesus which show the coming of the kingdom as a divinely violent happening in this world:

> Again the kingdom of heaven is like a dragnet cast into the sea that brings in a haul of all kinds. When it is full, the fishermen haul it ashore; then, sitting down, they collect the good ones in a basket and throw away those that are no use. This is how it will be at the end of time: the angels will appear and separate the wicked from the just to throw them into the blazing furnace where there will be weeping and grinding of teeth.
>
> (Matthew 13: 47-50)

But alongside these parables are others that speak of a kingdom not of this world. By the time John is writing, the phrase 'kingdom of God' has almost completely disappeared and in its one appearance has been transformed.

Nicodemus, the Pharisee who went to Jesus by night, was told by Jesus:

> 'I tell you most solemnly, unless a man is born from above, he cannot see the kingdom of God.'

Nicodemus said, 'How can a grown man be born? Can he go back into his mother's womb and be born again?' Jesus replied:

> 'I tell you most solemnly, unless a man is born through water and the Spirit, he cannot enter the kingdom of God: what is born of the flesh is flesh; what is born of the Spirit is spirit. Do not be surprised when I say: You must be born from above. The wind blows where it comes from or where it is going, That is how it is with all who are born of the Spirit.'
>
> (John 3: 3-8)

Instead of being a cosmic happening, the kingdom of God has come to mean eternal life, a spiritual rebirth. It is no longer of this world of flesh but of spirit, which cannot be judged by anything natural. For John, eternal life is not simply the life of the blessed in Heaven in the next world. It is the life of the spirit here and now which the Christian received at baptism, when Christ dwells in the soul of the convert. The kingdom of God, therefore, or as it becomes, 'eternal life', is not a future event but a present state. In John the next life is simply a continuation of what the Christian receives at baptism. In this theology we see the Christian answer to the failure of the eschatological hopes of the early Church. After AD 70 no such answer was possible for the Jewish Christians who sought to remain Jews.

Christianity prospered and grew in the Greco-Roman world. It survived the destruction of Jerusalem and established itself among the gentiles to become ultimately a gentile religion. But Paul, who had made the transplant, could never accept the break with Jerusalem. He tried for the rest of his life as a missionary to effect a reconciliation, and the Jewish rejection of his gospel filled him with sorrow. He could never give the Jews up and believed that finally they too would be saved. 'I have the very warmest love for the Jews,' he writes, 'and I pray to God for them to be saved' (Romans 10: 1):

> Let me put a further question then: Is it possible that *God has rejected his people*?[1] Of course not. I, an Israelite, descended from Abraham through the tribe of Benjamin, could never agree that God has rejected his people, the people he chose specially long ago.
>
> (Romans 11: 1-2)

The Jews are still the chosen people; through them salvation has come for the rest of the world. Their rejection of the gospel enabled God to turn to the gentiles so that they have been grafted on to the chosen people through their faith:

> The Jews are the enemies of God only with regard to the Good News, and enemies only for your sake; but as the Chosen People, they are still loved by God for the sake of their ancestors. God never takes back his gifts or revokes his choice.
>
> (Romans 11: 28-29)

Before the *parousia*, after the pagans have been evangelised, the Jews too will be converted; they too 'will enjoy mercy eventually' despite their former disobedience in rejecting Christ. They were after all the first recipients of the covenant.

On Paul's missionary journeys, his preaching in the synagogues caused havoc in the cities he visited, and he was persecuted and rejected by his own people. This is hardly surprising. His preaching that Israel's special mission was over would have been anathema. Paul, at Jerusalem and at Antioch, had started the inevitable parting of the ways between his Christianity and Judaism. For years after Paul's

1. Psalm 94: 14.

death Christians insisted that they were part of Judaism, that they were members of the local synagogue. They clung to Paul's teaching that they were the true Israel, and Christ the fulfilment of the Torah and the Prophets. But relations became increasingly strained. Matthew gives us some idea of what was going on in his account of Jesus' diatribe against the Pharisees:

> 'Serpents, brood of vipers, how can you escape being condemned to hell? This is why, in my turn, I am sending you prophets and wise men and scribes: some you will slaughter and crucify, some you will scourge in your synagogues and hunt from town to town; and so you will draw down upon yourselves the blood of every holy man that has been shed on earth, from the blood of Abel the Holy to the blood of Zechariah son of Barachiach whom you murdered between the sanctuary and the altar. I tell you solemnly, all of this will recoil on this generation.'
>
> (Matthew 23: 33-36)

Matthew, a converted Jew from the diaspora, shows the bitterness felt by these Jewish churches when they were rejected by their fellow Jews. It seems to have been unpleasant, with beatings and the sort of persecution Paul is said by Luke to have encountered on his travels, when he was pursued by Jews from town to town. There is a reference to the tension between Jews and Christians at this date at the end of the Beatitudes:

> 'Happy are you when people abuse you and persecute you and speak all kinds of calumny against you on my account. Rejoice and be glad, for your reward will be great in heaven; this is how they persecuted the prophets before you.'
>
> (Matthew 5: 11-12)

The Christian missionaries are seen as good Jews; they are, in Matthew's denunciation, 'prophets, wise men and scribes'. Yet their fellow Jews reject them violently. Matthew in his turn rejects the Jews as 'serpents and broods of vipers'. By AD 89, Christians were finally ejected from the synagogues and expelled from Judaism. The bad feeling engendered is seen in the anti-semitism of Matthew and John.

Paul must be given credit for not being anti-semitic, even though he suffered a great deal from the Jews. Quite the contrary, he maintained his love for his people and never gave up hope of their salvation. Paul is the first Christian in that he made Christianity into a gentile as opposed to a Jewish religion, but he is also the first Christian in that he gave to Christianity its major preoccupations and also some of its major problems. One legacy he bequeathed unwittingly to his successors arises out of his love of Judaism as the historical backcloth to Christianity.

One of the oldest of the holy places in Israel is the tomb of the patriarchs of Hebron. There, it is traditionally believed, Abraham and his wife Sarah are buried, together with Isaac and his son Jacob. The shrine was venerated in Paul's time as it is today, by Jews and Muslims, who also claim Abraham as their father. But Hebron is not only venerated because it is the resting place of the patriarchs, but also as the first significant worldly acquisition by the Hebrews.

When Sarah died at Kiriath-Arba or Hebron, Abraham went to the Canaanites after he had observed the due period of mourning:

Abraham spoke to the sons of Heth. 'I am a stranger and a settler among you,' he said. 'Let me own a burial plot among you, so that I may take my dead wife and bury her.' The sons of Heth gave Abraham this answer: 'Listen, my Lord, you are God's prince among us; bury your dead in the best of our tombs; not one of us would refuse you his tomb and keep you from burying your dead.'

Abraham rose and bowed to the ground before the people of the land, he spoke to the sons of Heth. 'If', he said, 'you are willing for me to take my dead wife and bury her, then listen to me. Intercede for me with Ephron, Zohar's son, to

give me the cave he owns at Machpelah, which is on the edge
of his land. Let him make it over to me in your presence at its
full price, for me to own as a burial plot.' Now Ephron was
sitting among the sons of Heth and Ephron the Hittite
answered Abraham in the hearing of the sons of Heth and of
all the citizens of the town. 'My lord, listen to me,' he said. 'I
give you the land and I give you the cave on it; I make this gift
in the sight of the sons of my people. Bury your dead.'

Abraham bowed before the people of the land and he
spoke to Ephron in the hearing of the people of the land,
'Oh, if it be you . . . But listen to me. I will pay the price of
the land; accept it from me and I will bury my dead there.'
Ephron answered Abraham, 'My lord, listen to me. A
property worth four hundred shekels of silver, what is a little
thing like that between me and you? Bury your dead.'
Abraham agreed to Ephron's terms, and Abraham weighed
out for Ephron the silver he had stipulated in the hearing of
the sons of Heth, namely four hundred shekels of silver,
according to the current commercial rate.

Thus Ephron's field at Machpelah opposite Mamre, the
field and the cave that was on it, and all the trees that were on
it, the whole of its extent in every direction, passed into
Abraham's possession in the sight of the sons of Heth, and of
all the citizens of the town. After this Abraham buried his
wife Sarah in the cave of the field of Machpelah opposite
Mamre, namely Hebron, in the country of Canaan. And so
the field and the cave that was on it passed from the sons of
Heth into Abraham's possession to be owned as a burial
plot.

(Genesis 23)

This narrative would never have found its way into a
Christian scripture and it shows us so clearly what Judaism
is about, and how it differs from Christianity. Hebron is the
first piece of land in Judaea that the Jews acquired. When
Abraham managed to buy that cave, God's promise to him
that he would own the whole land of Canaan was beginning
to be fulfilled. The deal is recounted by the priestly author
of Genesis in minute detail. The Hittites try to press the land

Paul, apostle to the gentiles. 'The fact is, brothers, and I want you to realise this, the Good News I preached is not a human message that I was given by men, it is something I learnt only through a revelation of Jesus Christ' (Galatians 1:11). St Paul is depicted here on an English orphrey, dated *c.* 1300, in the Victoria and Albert Museum

'I am a Jew,' Paul said, 'and was born at Tarsus in Cilicia' (Acts 22:3). An engraving of Tarsus by W. H. Bartlett, 1840

Pious Jews traditionally retreated to the desert for periods of purification. Immediately after his conversion, Paul, too, withdrew to the deserts of Arabia

The nomadic bedouin in the desert would have symbolised for Paul the transitory nature of the 'last days'. 'For we know that when the tent that we live in on earth has folded up, there is a home built by God for us, an everlasting home' (2 Corinthians 5:1)

With Paul's violent vision on the road to Damascus, Christianity as we know it was born. This depiction of the conversion is from a nineteenth-century stained-glass window in Lincoln Cathedral

The parable of the Pharisee and the publican sums up the complacency of the Pharisees as they are depicted in the gospels. This stained-glass window in Lincoln Cathedral illustrates the parable

St Peter, whom Paul publicly accused at Antioch of adopting double standards. 'In spite of being a Jew, you live like the pagans and not like the Jews, so you have no right to make the pagans copy Jewish ways' (Galatians 2:14). This portrait is from the thirteenth-century Westminster retable, Westminster Abbey

above left: Throughout his missionary life, Paul wanted the gentile churches to maintain their historic link with Jerusalem, the holy city, shown here from the Mount of Olives

below left: For the Jew, study of the Law of Moses has always been a means of intimacy with God. A Jewish student at prayer on a rooftop in Jerusalem

St Luke, the probable travelling companion of Paul, and his biographer in
Acts of the Apostles, is also the evangelist who most closely follows Paul's
theology. St Paul and St Luke are shown here in detail from the Communion
of the Apostles, Church of the Holy Cross, Platanistasa, Cyprus

above right: In Macedonia, Paul travelled along the *Via Egnatia*, which
linked the eastern provinces of the empire with Rome itself

below right: The traditional view of the composition of the gospels:
St Matthew and St Luke work closely together, directly inspired from
Heaven. This is a fifteenth-century mural of the two in the Church of
the Holy Cross, Platanistasa, Cyprus

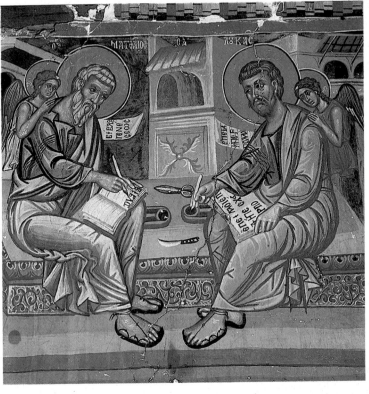

Although he is often accused of an unaesthetic realism, Grunewald preserves
something of the shock that the Cross would have been to Paul's converts.
This Crucifixion is from the Isenheim altarpiece

on Abraham as a gift, but with immense Oriental courtesy, Abraham refuses. It is important for him to own the land, to pay for it and for his ownership to be witnessed by the people of Heth. Only thus can Abraham, the nomad, 'a stranger and settler' among the people who now own the land, be recognised as a full inhabitant, with legal and landed rights. He pays for his cave 'at the current commercial rate'. He refuses to accept charity, however courteously it is pressed upon him. The first piece of Jewish land in Canaan was properly purchased by the patriarch, with a bargain made between equals.

Judaism is a religion of this world. It is based on a specific piece of land, and ownership of that land was – and still is – of crucial importance. The Jewish Christians also believed in a kingdom of this world. Of course they would agree with Paul that when Christ came again in glory it would be a cosmic event, that the present world would be transformed, but Jesus would come as a Jewish Messiah and the kingdom of God would be centred in Israel.

What Paul did for Christianity was to take it right out of this world. Because the political element in Paul's gospel was thus weakened, Christianity became a religion concerned far more with sin, with eternal life, with mystical dying in the death of Jesus and the attainment of freedom from the fetters of sin and death. Even Jesus' life on earth, as we have seen, was for Paul an irrelevant issue: 'If we once knew Jesus as he was when he was in the flesh, that is not how we know him any longer' (2 Corinthians 5: 16). The death and resurrection had plunged Jesus and all Christians into a wholly new element, a new reality.

Under the influence of Paul, the evangelists make Jesus utter remarks to the effect that his kingdom is not of this world; in the Sermon on the Mount, Matthew has Jesus abandon anxiety about possessions and earthly necessities. Christians reading the account of Abraham's purchase of the cave at Hebron could experience distaste at the delight taken in the commercial procedure. This is not 'spiritual' enough for religion, they may feel, which should be above all such transactions; whereas for the Jew the commercial details are religious because their religion is not only about God but about this world too. Yet Paul wanted Judaism; he also wanted history. As we shall see, he took care to found a religion which was embedded firmly in the very real world of Rome and the empire. He would make Christianity reject the world and yet he was a man of sound efficiency and practical sense. He knew that nobody could stand out against the Roman Empire, and while Paul had a hearty disgust for Roman decadence and the Roman lifestyle, he passionately admired Roman administration and urged his followers to support it wholeheartedly.

There is a paradox here, and paradox is something that we find in Paul again and again. Christianity looks away from this world to a mystical union with Christ. However, it also seeks a link, historical and political, with the world. Today we find in Christianity institutions which all claim to be naked following the naked Christ in a daily crucifixion, but which are in fact sophisticated organisations, riddled with internal and external politics. The recent scandal of the Vatican bank is a very odd affair in an institution vowed to poverty of spirit, and the wealth of the Vatican is a strange phenomenon in a Church whose founder told his followers to sell all they had and give the money to the poor. But the Church of England's position in the English establishment is equally ambiguous for a religion that seeks a kingdom not of this world. Many members of the Church of England find it increasingly difficult morally to support government policy, and yet they know that to cease to be part of the establishment would mean the Church's bankruptcy. This paradox bedevils Christianity, not only at the top level. The average parishioner, who listens to a gospel in which Jesus asks his followers to leave their possessions, their wives, their families and all that they have for his sake, must feel a twinge of unease as he leaves the church to go home to a Sunday lunch with his family, to a house which he is paying for by monthly instalments, and with the thought of his job and career recommencing on Monday morning.

Paul enjoyed paradox. He was a clever man and it cannot be too strongly stressed that for him temporal existence was coming to an end. Christ would return soon in glory; these were the 'last days', it was a time of crisis and emergency. During crisis, paradox is the order of the day. Only when paradox is extended indefinitely, in this case for two thousand years, can it become schizophrenia. Without realising it, Paul bequeathed to Christianity its schizophrenic perspective. 'In the world but not of it' is an inspiring maxim, but one almost impossible to live by in practice. Abraham's purchasing of his burial plot, an acquisition which embedded his religion and race in history, was something that Paul tried to do himself *vis à vis* the Roman Empire. Paul liked Abraham, who was a useful figure for him in his polemic against the Jewish Christians. Abraham, scripture says, 'was justified by his faith', and that, Paul adds triumphantly, was *before* he was circumcised (Romans 4: 9-11). Luther, reading the Epistle to the Galatians, discovered the whole of Protestantism in that one phrase (Galatians 3: 6) and probably gave to the notion of justification by faith a prominence and significance which it does not possess in Paul's thought.

What does Paul mean by faith? He does not mean an intellectual assent to a set of dogmas. That is what we often mean when we talk about faith today, but Paul uses the term not in the sense of intellectual belief at all, but as we use the word 'trust'. Abraham had faith in God, not because he believed that he existed and believed certain things about him, but because he trusted God, he believed in his promises even when things seemed hopeless:

> Though it seemed Abraham's hope could not be fulfilled he hoped and he believed, and through doing so he did become

the father of many nations[1] exactly as he had been promised: *your descendants will be as many as the stars*[2] Even the thought that his body was past fatherhood – he was about a hundred years old – and Sarah too old to become a mother, did not shake his belief. Since God had promised it, Abraham refused either to deny it or even to doubt it, but drew strength from faith and gave glory to God convinced that God had power to do what he had promised. This is the faith which was *considered as justifying him.*[3]

(Romans 4: 18-22)

Genesis tells a nice story about Sarah. When Abraham was entertaining the three strangers at Mamre, in what appears to have been some mysterious divine visitation, they prophesied that Sarah would shortly conceive. Sarah had been eavesdropping behind the tent-flap and found the whole idea so ridiculous –she was long past the menopause – that she burst out laughing and betrayed her whereabouts (18: 9-15). The laughter of Sarah is important. Like Abraham's faith, Paul's faith was in some sense ridiculous. The belief that an ordinary, sordid crucifixion had power to redeem the whole world is not a reasonable expectation. That is why Paul insists that the Christian must have the same faith as Abraham; his faith in God's power to release him from sin and death is absurd. Any efforts by Christians to lessen the absurdity of their faith, any apologetics seeking to explain it in terms of reason, any whittling down of the fundamental incredibility of belief in God and the gospel, has nothing to do with the faith of Paul.

Abraham's greatest test of faith came when God commanded him to sacrifice his son, Isaac, even though God had promised that it was through Isaac's line, that the promise would descend to Abraham's descendants. This gives some indication of what faith meant to Paul. To define faith, as we

1. Genesis 17:5.
2. Genesis 15:5.
3. Genesis 15:6.

usually do today, as intellectual orthodoxy runs against the notion of God as transcendent. Judaism insisted on identity of practice but not on identity of belief. Provided that the Torah was obeyed, you could more or less believe what you liked about God, because God was always bigger than any one man's vision. When God appeared to Moses in the burning bush and told him to go to the Children of Israel on his behalf, Moses asked God for his name. In the ancient Semitic world to know the name of someone meant that they were in your power. To know the name of a God meant that you had defined him and could make him do what you wanted. When Moses asked God for his name, God replied: 'I am who I am' usually translated 'I am who am' (Exodus 3: 14). Christians, usually with a training in Greek habits of rational and analytical thought, have interpreted this to mean that God is saying that he is self-subsistent being, but such a concept would have been foreign to the concrete mode of thought of the ancient Semites. God is using a Hebrew idiom of deliberate vagueness. 'They went where they went' means 'I haven't a clue where they went.' Similarly, 'I am who I am' means 'Never you mind who I am.' The God of Israel cannot be defined or controlled by man.

Christians have lost this sense of God's transcendence in their concern to impose identity of belief on their subjects. All sects have done it: you must believe thus and thus about God in order to be saved. Only if you believe what the Pope, what Luther or Calvin or Cranmer, decrees can you be justified. This limits God to the capacity of individual human minds; God is created according to a man's image and likeness or to the image and likeness of a particular historical period with its own needs and preoccupations. People often say that their faith gives them a security in a shifting and troubling world. This has nothing to do with the faith of Abraham, which is what Paul insists is the only thing that can justify mankind. Christians who can believe exactly what they are told feel secure; not only have they abandoned intellectual responsibility and the agonies of doubt, but they have also cut God down to the size of a human system. God commanded Abraham to plunge a knife into the breast of his only and dearly loved son. He was commanding him to go beyond what a human being can think acceptable or right. God, who so far exceeds us, can be a very nasty shock indeed to our limited human selves. Paul in effect is saying that the Christian faith does not always produce security but can bring all the terror of the irrational and the absurd. In Christianity we are led out of the safety of what the world thinks acceptable into a new and possibly alarming world. 'It is a dreadful thing,' says Paul's disciple, the author of the Epistle to the Hebrews, 'to fall into the hands of the living God' (10: 31). In coming to define faith as intellectual assent, Christianity has offended the concept of a wholly mysterious and transcendent God and has not been true to the God of Judaism, which it claims is the same as its own, nor to the vision of the first Christian.

The rejection of Christianity by Judaism was one of the first and most difficult problems the early Church had to face. The Church has accepted Luke's edifying picture of Peter and Paul as the united pillars of the Church: Peter, apostle to the Jews, and Paul, apostle to the gentiles. They are often depicted side by side, Paul with his sword and Peter with his keys. Yet we have seen that the early Church was split in a very ugly conflict. Its bitterness runs through Paul's letters: 'Watch out for the cutters!' he writes (Philippians 3: 3) of the Jewish Christians who still insist on circumcision. Or: 'Tell those who are disturbing you that I should like to see the knife slip' (Galatians 5: 12). Paul's stand on circumcision would eventually sever the Church from Judaism.

In the course of his missionary journeys Paul suffered much from the Jews. His preaching offended them and they retaliated violently. In Acts they are continually driving him out of town, getting him imprisoned, beating him up. Yet Paul himself, with an admirable loyalty never rejected Judaism. The same cannot be said of later Christians. The gospels of Matthew and John, springing from predominantly Jewish churches, retaliate with virulent anti-semitism to the abuse the evangelists endured in the synagogues. That was only the beginning of Christian anti-semitism, which grew steadily in the first centuries of Christianity. Christians were urged by theologians and preachers like St John Chrysostom to shun Jews, the God-slayers. 'Chrysostom' means 'golden-mouthed', a nick-name given to John for his eloquence, but his anti-semitic utterances are foul-mouthed in the extreme.

Anti-semistism reached a peak during the Middle Ages. We see it clearly in stories like 'The Prioress' Tale' in *The Canterbury Tales*, with its depiction of Jews murdering little children. Nor is this a thing of the distant past. It was possible for Pope Pius XII, the successor of the Jewish Peter, not to condemn the Nazis. Even the Vatican council, in its embarrassed acknowledgement of Christianity's bad record here, asserts that the Jews can be exonerated only if they reject the generation that killed Jesus. Apart from the fact that it was most unlikely that the Jews were responsible for the death of Christ, Hyam Maccoby has recently pointed out that the 'generation' that lived at the time of Jesus was the richest generation of scholars that Judaism has ever known. Asking Judaism to disown it is like asking Christianity to disown the period of the fathers of the Church. In this tide of Christian anti-semitism Paul has often been called in to support the Jew-baiters. However, this is to mistake him entirely. Paul's writings against the Law, his angry polemics in Galatians and elsewhere, are not directed against the Jews but against the Jewish Christians, who were denying the basic tenets of his gospel. Paul remained all his life, as far as we know, a lifelong lover of Judaism.

4 In the world but not of it

After the council of Jerusalem, Paul set off on his second great missionary journey. The dispute at Antioch catapulted him away from the world of Judaism. Barnabas, the companion of his first missionary journey, had sided with Peter and James, refusing to work any longer with him. Silas now accompanied him, and from the letters we gather that his two other missionary companions were the half-Jewish Timothy and the uncircumcised Titus. For years Antioch had been Paul's base. Now he no longer seems to have a base in the Jewish-Christian world. But for all this, Judaism remained Paul's spiritual home; the Jews were his 'flesh and blood'. When he set out again into the gentile world, he must have felt himself a exile, as we can infer in the Epistles. Paul's personal sense of exile would affect his gospel and stamp on Christianity a sense of exile from the world.

Paul's original brief, according to Luke, was to revisit the churches he had established in Asia Minor and on Cyprus. Constantly in his travels Paul was concerned to keep the brothers on the right lines. We owe the Epistles to the problems that these infant churches encountered and to Paul's firm guidance and concern that they keep faithful to his original gospel. He felt a great sense of urgency to move out, to preach the gospel 'to the ends of the earth'. Before Christ returned he had an immense task to perform. Yet the forward thrust of his mission was constantly impeded by disputes and difficulties, and there was the endless task of straightening out muddles and healing conflicts that any new community has to face.

He travelled through Syria and Asia Minor for about one thousand miles. Paul gives us some indication of the hardship of these journeys: 'We prove we are servants of God by great fortitude in times of hardship or distress . . . when we are labouring, sleepless, starving' (2 Corinthians 5: 5–6). He had perils not only from the elements and the natural dangers of inhospitable country, but also from persecution by the Jews and indeed by his fellow believers. Luke gives us some examples in Acts of the Apostles, but Paul's is an even more heroic record:

> I have been sent to prison . . . and whipped so many times . . . often almost to death. Five times I had the thirty-nine lashes from the Jews; three times I have been beaten with sticks; once I was stoned; three times I have been shipwrecked and once adrift in the open sea for a night and a day. Constantly travelling, I have been in peril from rivers and in danger from brigands, in danger from my own people and in danger from pagans; in danger in the towns, in danger in the open country, danger at sea and danger from so-called brothers. I have worked and laboured often without sleep; I have been hungry and thirsty and often starving; I have been in the cold without clothes. And to leave out much more, there is my daily preoccupation: my anxiety for all the churches. When any man has had scruples, I have had scruples with him; when any man is made to fall, I am tortured.
>
> (2 Corinthians 11: 23–29)

The tenacity and courage displayed here are admirable. Paul is writing to a church which was forsaking its allegiance to him and siding with more apparently successful apostles, who did not look so bedraggled and hard-pressed. As he develops his argument, he is building up a new concept: that of Christian suffering. These trials are the Christian's way of entering into the death of Jesus. Paul is a servant of Christ, more so than these other, more worldly apostles, precisely because he suffers more, precisely because he has been to prison more frequently, been beaten more severely. It is part of the faith which made Abraham ready to kill his own son; the gospel of Christ leads the Christian away from worldly happiness and earthly preconceptions.

We are now entering into the period of the great Epistles, all written during the 50s. This passage is a good example of the way Paul develops his theology – in the midst of hardship and crisis and in answer to a specific problem. In the last chapter of this book we shall see what later Christians have made of Paul's doctrine of suffering. The gusto with which he boasts of his sufferings here is for a specific purpose – to shame the Corinthians into a true appreciation of the meaning of the Cross. It is sufficient now to notice that Paul's chosen life of hardship is removing the gospel away from the world with which we are familiar.

After revisiting the churches in Asia Minor, Paul, as we know from his letters, travelled north into Galatia, where he founded the Galatian church. Here, not surprisingly after such a lengthy journey, he fell ill with a disease which many would have thought 'revolting' and 'disgusting', as he reminds them later. It is this church which would later fall prey to the Judaising Christians, and to whom Paul would write his great letter of polemic.

Paul continued across Asia Minor and arrived at Troas, where he had one of his visions. Luke records it in Acts, and it is at this point in the narrative that he starts to write in the first person plural, as though he had now joined Paul as one of his travelling companions. Some scholars have argued that the third person was a commonly used device to give vividness to a narrative. It is also true that Luke is an ardent champion of Paul's, and of all the evangelists has adopted the most thorough Paulinism. It may well be that he did travel with Paul for a time:

> A Macedonian appeared and appealed to him [Paul] in these words, 'Come across to Macedonia and help us.' Once he had seen this vision we lost no time in arranging a passage to Macedonia, convinced that God had called us to bring them the good news.
>
> (Acts 16: 9–10)

This sounds like a story that has become familiar to us through reading biographies of the Christian saints. There is a vision, and on the strength of that all plans are changed and the whole party sets off for Macedonia. Paul had to preach to the whole of the gentile world. Why should the Macedonians be in more urgent need than any of the other pagan nations?

They weren't. These visions recounted by Luke often herald a concerted and well-thought-out policy. Paul always tethers his other-worldy visions firmly to the real world. We saw that he went to Jerusalem to confront James and Peter on the circumcision question 'as the result of a revelation' (Galatians 2: 2), but not in a vague or visionary way; he had conceived the effective policy of taking with him the uncircumcised Titus. Similarly, he did not wander moonily off to Macedonia on a mystical whim. There was a clear and ambitious policy behind his change of direction. If Paul did suffer from epilepsy or another neurological illness, perhaps these visions, when the brain was temporarily convulsed, clarified issues for him. He had, remember, recently been ill in Galatia.

Paul was convinced that he had a mission to evangelise the whole world, but he was not foolhardy enough to think that he could preach the gospel to every nation single-handed. Every church he set up was to be a missionary centre for future evangelising of the surrounding countryside. He now set off, via Macedonia, to Europe, to penetrate the Roman empire more thoroughly. If he crossed to Macedonia from Troas, he would land at Neapolis, modern Cavalla. At nearby Philippi he could join the great Via Egnatia which cut across south-east Europe to Illyricum and, on the other side of the Adriatic, became the Via Appia, leading directly to Rome. The vision of the Macedonian may have been Paul's moment of realisation that by far the most effective missionary centre of all was Rome, the centre of the empire and the world. Later he learned that a church had already been established at Rome, and he wrote it a letter, his great theological manifesto. Here he frequently expresses his desire to visit Rome; he would have wanted to be certain that they had his gospel, not that of any of the other apostles, as this was such a potentially important church. From Rome, he told the Christians there, he intended to go across to Spain, where the Pillars of Hercules marked what was then believed to be the ends of the earth (Roman 15: 23 ff.). Once he had preached there, Paul's mission would be accomplished and it would be time for the *parousia*.

It is interesting to see where Paul established churches when he had crossed into Europe. Macedonia, which had once been great under Alexander, was now only a defeated province of the Roman Empire. Once Paul landed on European soil, he made straight for Philippi and it was here that the first European church, as far as we know, was established. Philippi was the scene of the battle of 42 BC, when Mark Antony defeated Brutus and Cassius, avenging the murder of Julius Caesar. To celebrate his victory, Anotny granted Philippi the *ius Italicum*, the privilege of a Roman city. Paul, then, set up his first church in Europe in a Roman city. Philippi was to be the missionary centre for Macedonia, and Paul's letter to the Philippians is one of his most personal and affectionate Epistles. He wanted to work alongside the empire, not oppose it, establishing Christianity in the administrative centres of Rome. As a Roman citizen, he had none of the Judaean Jews' antipathy to Rome which perhaps Jesus himself shared. As an intelligent man he knew very well the empire's power. If you wanted to evangelise the pagan world, you had to go along with the empire.

Later Christians would accept Paul's vision of an empire-based Church. For centuries Christendom was ruled entirely by the 'bishop' of Rome, who controlled what became known as the Holy Roman Empire. In fact the great problem of the medieval Church was its entanglement with the secular arm. Even the way the Church was set up, with bishops and archbishops ruling the various dioceses like provinces under the lead of Rome, is reminiscent of the empire. Of course, all this was far in the future, but the involvement of the Church with the political world was originally Paul's vision. He had no idea of the problems that would result, but was simply trying to fulfil his missionary brief in the most effective way possible. He was far more interested, for example, in founding a church in Corinth, the Roman capital of Achaia, than in establishing Christianity in the cultural centre of Athens. Culture, we shall see, was not Paul's strong point.

Just as Paul wanted to preserve Christianity's links with history through Judaism, he wanted to use Rome to make sure that his missionary journeys were effective. He never thought of going to the northern parts of Europe, for example, nor to Britain. From the Roman centres, from Rome itself, other evangelists could take his gospel into the remote reaches of the empire.

We are entirely dependent on Acts for the story of the establishment of the Philippian church. It is a legendary account. Apparently Paul cast out the 'devil' of a slave-girl who was a successful fortune-teller. Her owners, who had

found her talents lucrative, were understandably put out
and dragged Paul off before the magistrates, where he was
accused of disturbing the peace. In prison, Luke says, there
was an earthquake which opened the doors of the prison.
Paul's honourable behaviour in not escaping converted the
gaoler on the spot. Paul himself, writing to the Thessalonians, does not mention the prison episode, nor the
apology of the magistrates when they learn that he was a
Roman citizen. He speaks only of 'suffering and shameful
treatment' at Philippi (1 Thessalonians 2: 2). However,
when Luke says that he used his Roman citizenship with the
authorities to get out of prison, he is probably correct. It
would be part of Paul's policy of cooperation; he would
have wanted the Romans to see that the new sect was in no
way subversive. There was no question at this date of
Christianity being illegal. Chrisitanity was still technically
part of Judaism and thus enjoyed the religious freedom
Rome afforded the Jews. However, Paul wanted more than
toleration from Rome. He wanted support.

From Rome, Paul made his way to Thessalonika, another
centre of Roman administration. It was the capital city of
Macedonia and the seat of a proconsul, thus admirably
suited as one of Paul's missionary centres. At Thessalonika,
Luke says, he encountered enormous hostility from the
Jews, 'who, full of resentment, enlisted the help of a gang
from the market-place, stirred up a crowd, and soon had the
whole city in an uproar' (Acts 17: 5). They managed to gain
the support of the authorities with the accusation that Paul
and Silas 'had broken every one of Caesar's edicts by
claiming that there is another emperor, Jesus' (Acts 17: 7).
Paul and Silas were smuggled ignominiously out of town
and hastened to nearby Beroea.

Luke has truncated the story of Paul's stay in Thessalonika, as in his letter to the Church there it is obvious
that he stayed for some months. It was a strong church in

Thessalonika. In Corinth he heard that the Thessalonians were suffering great persecution and he wrote warmly to them, congratulating them on their fidelity and courage. It also appears that they were taking their task as missionaries very seriously. Such suffering, Paul writes, 'has made you the great example to all believers in Macedonia and Achaia since it was from you that the word of the Lord started to spread – and not only throughout Macedonia and Achaia, for the news of your faith in God has spread everywhere' (1 Thessalonians 1: 7-8). It seems to have been predominantly a gentile church; Paul reminds them how they 'broke with idolatry to serve the real living God' (1 Thessalonians 1: 9).

This was an age intensely interested in religion. People were seeking new religious answers and that inevitably meant a good deal of religious rivalry. Paul was not the only itinerant preacher on the road. He would have had to contend with pagan apostles claiming a divine mission and boasting about the sufferings they had undergone or flamboyantly displaying their gifts and spiritual wisdom to show the superiority of their god or cult. In view of this, Paul reminds the Thessalonians, it is amazing that his Christian converts took him seriously at all. Instead of cutting an impressive figure, Paul arrived very much the worse for wear after being given 'rough treatment and having been grossly insulted at Philippi' (1 Thessalonians 2: 2), and encountering great opposition in Thessalonika itself. By sheer force of circumstance he was developing in this earliest Epistle his doctrine of the other-worldliness of Christianity. The worldly methods of the pagan apostles are shown to be less impressive than the power of the gospel with its unsuccessful and unflamboyant apostle, Paul.

When he fled to Beroea, where the Thessalonikan Jews got him evicted quite smartly, Paul had left the Via Egnatia. It may have been part of his intention to evangelise the Roman province of Achaia by visiting Corinth, or perhaps

the persecutions he suffered in Thessalonika and Beroea
threw him off course, so that he had to head south-west
towards Athens, abandoning his original intention of going
straight to Rome.

At all events, Paul arrived in Athens. After the trauma of
the journey he had endured so far, even as Luke tells it, he
must have been feeling bruised and battered emotionally
and physically. He had journeyed through perilous country
for hundreds of miles; he had been imprisoned twice at least,
been set upon by gangs, been seriously ill in Galatia. He had
also encountered the rivalry of the more cunning and
sophisticated pagan apostles. Commending the Thessalonians for seeing the gospel as it really was, despite the
poor show that he had to put up, he writes:

> We have not taken to preaching because we are deluded, or
> immoral, or trying to deceive anyone; it was God who
> decided that we were fit to be entrusted with the Good
> News, and when we are speaking, we are not trying to please
> men but God, *who can read our inmost thoughts.*[1] You know
> very well, and we can swear it before God, that never at any
> time have our speeches been simply flattery, or a cover for
> trying to get money, nor have we ever looked for any special
> honour from men, either from you or anybody else, when
> we could have imposed ourselves on you with full weight, as
> apostles of Christ.
>
> (1 Thessalonians 2: 3-7)

The implication is that the pagan apostles of other cults were
appealing to the standards of the world, not merely finan-
cially, but also using vulgar methods of flattery and
prestige-seeking. Paul must have felt increasingly a division
between the gospel of Christ and the way of the world. He
can have been in no mood to encounter the cultural sophis-
tication of Athens, even though Athens was long past its

1 Jeremiah 11: 20.

former glories and was now as disregarded as Paul himself.

It is a commonplace that if Rome conquered Athens politically, Athens had conquered Rome more subtly in a cultural *coup*. Rome had adopted and romanised the Olympian heirarchy of gods; Rome, without much of its own intellectual life, had adopted the great achievements of Athens in philosophy and metaphysics. In Athens, even if he looked no further than the architecture and sculpture surrounding him, Paul encountered all that was finest in the ancient world. He rejected it as superfluous, indeed antagonistic, to his gospel.

Luke gives an account of Paul's visit to Athens as a glorious and triumphant failure. He has Paul preaching on the Areopagus and arguing with the Greeks like a Greek philosopher, using their methods and presenting Christ to them in their terms. The truth must have been very different. As we have seen, though Paul grew up a Greek speaker in the free Greek city of Tarsus, he was no real Hellene. Plato and Aristotle seem to have passed him by, let alone the more obscure branches of Greek culture. As a conscientious Jew, whose religion forbade the making of graven images, he would probably have disapproved of Greek sculpture, and there is no hint that he knew any of the Greek literature and drama, nor about the religious world of the Greeks. How then was he going to preach his Judaic message to the sophisticated Athenians, who would consider his teaching barbaric?

Paul shows, in his letters, that he felt no diffidence in approaching the seat of ancient learning. We have seen that his vision spoke to him with such authority when he was converted that he felt no need to discuss it with any of the people who had been apostles before him, and during the circumcision conflict he had been contemptuous of the seniority of Peter and James. He felt equally confident in Greece, confronted with its superior culture:

As for me, brothers, when I came to you, it was not with any show of oratory or philosophy, but simply to tell you what God had guaranteed. During my stay with you, the only knowledge I claimed to have was about Jesus, and only about him as a crucified Christ. Far from relying on any power of my own, I came among you in great 'fear and trembling' and in my speeches and sermons that I gave, there were none of the arguments that belong to philosophy; only a demonstration of the power of the Spirit. And I did this so that your faith should not depend on human philosophy but on the power of God.

(1 Corinthians 2: 1-5)

There was no attempt on Paul's part, even if he had been equipped to do so, to use Greek culture or philosophy to further his message. Rather, he is proud of the fact that he shows no human skill, relies on no human wisdom at all, unlike the pagan apostles he encountered in Thessalonika.

Paul is right. He was preaching, as he reminds the Corinthians, the gospel of the crucified Messiah and 'the crucifixion of Christ cannot be expressed in terms of philosophy' (1 Corinthians 1: 17). The Crucifixion is an overturning of every single natural human value, and it would have been even more striking then than it has been for the many generations of Christians since, because the Cross has become acceptable to us through so many paintings and sculptures that depict it as symbolic of an event of great beauty. Too many literary works have done the same. The Cross is a household image; we are accustomed to seeing it everywhere, topping steeples and adorning young girls' necks on dainty silver chains. The shock value of the Cross has completely disappeared, and over-familiarity with its doctrine means that preachers today have to burst a blood vessel to try to get their flocks to see it for the enormity it represents. This, Christianity says, is what God means by love and by victory, an overturning of all human expectations. Seen like this – a man dying by one of the most painful tortures ever devised – the Cross should speak of the transcendence of God, a transcendence that is so clear in the Old Testament.

> For my thoughts are not your thoughts, my ways not your ways – it is Yahweh who speaks. Yes, the heavens are as high above the earth as my ways are above your ways, my thoughts above your thoughts.
>
> (Isaiah 55: 8-9)

Paul was spared this modern problem. The Cross was not a work of art to his converts, but a horrible and shocking reality. To go to the sophisticated world of the Greeks and tell them that the Cross was 'the power and wisdom of God' revealed on earth must have seemed madness; indeed, to the Greeks the Cross can only be 'madness' (1 Corinthians 1: 25). Today it would be equivalent to a preacher showing a man in the extremities of being hanged, drawn and quartered or showing a body blown to bits by a bomb and saying that that is what God is about; a shock to the system now, just as God had been a shock to Abraham's system when he ordered him to sacrifice his only son.

The utter folly of his message was to Paul a vindication of his life since his conversion, with its sufferings and persecutions. Human wisdom and rationality had no part in his conversion, as we have seen, and they could have no part in the conversion of his disciples. The world, whether the world of Judaism or the world of the Greeks, as he had learned bitterly at Antioch, at Philippi and at Thessalonika, could only be inimical to the Cross:

> The language of the cross may be illogical to those who are not on the way to salvation, but those of us who are on the way see it as God's power to save. As scripture says: *I shall destroy the wisdom of the wise and bring to nothing all the*

learning of the learned.[1] *Where are the philosophers now?*[2]
Where are the scribes?[3] Where are any of our thinkers today?
Do you see now how God has shown up the foolishness of
human wisdom?

(1 Corinthians 1: 18-21)

For Paul, 'God's foolishness' in the Cross 'is wiser than
human wisdom, and God's weakness is stronger than
human strength' (1 Corinthians 1: 25). This is evidenced by
the fact that his converts in Corinth were simple and
uneducated people, neither wise nor successful by the
world's standards. It puts clever, worldly people to shame.
Human wisdom is of no help in approaching the Cross of
Christ.

Paul's attitude is understandable. Like Christ, who had
preached only to the lost sheep of Israel, and whose following in Galilee seems largely to have been from the poorer
classes, so Paul, clever and learned as he was, got a hearing in
Corinth largely among the poor. Yet what about Christians
who, for no fault of their own, may have received, for
example, an expensive education? What about people whose
ambiguous experience in the world makes it difficult for
them to accept the Christian message? It is sometimes hard
to lay aside the intellectual and logical habits of a lifetime
and take a deliberate leap into pure irrationality. What it
often means in practice is that we diminish the less-credible
aspects of Christianity and create for ourselves our own
rational version, with a God in our own image and likeness.
Or, if we belong to a church that insists on uniformity of
belief, we have to tiptoe gingerly round difficult articles of
faith, never engaging with them honestly for fear our faith
will crumble away. We do not bring our whole selves to our
religion.

1. Isaiah 29:14.
2. Isaiah 33:18 (Paul quotes from the Septuagint not the Hebrew
text).
3. Isaiah 19:12.

For Paul and for many of his converts in his enthusiastic churches – I use the word 'enthusiasm' here in its original sense, meaning inspired by the spirit – faith was less of a problem. People had visions; they felt themselves taken over by God in such powerful ways that rational doubt became irrelevant; they and their fellow Christians 'spoke in tongues' and worked miracles. But for those of us who have not been privileged with vision, faith is more difficult. Perhaps we can only preserve our faith by abandoning our intellectual integrity. When reading passages like the following, many honest Christians must feel an uneasiness:

> Make no mistake about it: if any one of you thinks of himself as wise, in the ordinary sense of the word, then he must learn to be a fool before he really can be wise. Why? Because the wisdom of this world is foolishness to God. As scripture says: *The Lord knows wise men's thoughts: he knows how useless they are;*[1] or again: *God is not convinced by the arguments of the wise.*[2] So there is nothing to boast about in anything human.

(1 Corinthians 3: 18-22)

Can anybody who has encountered the powers and sensitivity of the human mind at its best endorse the last sentence? Are all men's thoughts – Einstein's, Pasteur's, Plato's – 'useless'?

The Parthenon in Athens was dedicated to Athena, one of whose attributes was goddess of wisdom. This should suggest that not all human wisdom is useless; some of it can be divinely inspired. Paul would perhaps have scarcely thrown the Parthenon a second glance; he was little impressed by the culture it had come to symbolise. His attitude here – understandable though it may be – flung Christendom into the Dark Ages, by denying human

1. Psalms 94: 11.
2. Job 5: 13.

achievements of learning and culture, even though it must be said that Luther's rediscovery of Paul helped pull Europe into the modern period. Leaving aside these broad historical implications, haven't we all met Christians who use the teaching of Paul to adopt a contrived philistinism, a denial of intellect and culture, that makes a great display of humility but is in fact a thin disguise for smug superiority? Then there are the fundamentalists, who refuse to look at Biblical criticism. Thus they distort the truth of the Bible, by neglecting the methods which could elucidate the spirit in which it was written. At the opposite pole, the only infallible papal pronouncement that the Roman Catholic Church has made since infallibility was made an article of faith in 1870 is a declaration that the Blessed Virgin Mary was assumed body and soul into Heaven on her death. It is very difficult for a Catholic honestly to believe that somewhere, floating in the heavens, is the body of a woman who died 2,000 years ago; it is equally difficult to see why such an inessential doctrine should now be binding and essential for salvation to all Catholics. Again, the Catholic teaching on contraception goes against all charity, all wisdom, but it is an assertion of 'God's foolishness' in face of the wisdom of the world. In all these Christian attitudes we have the same swagger that we noticed in Paul. But whereas with him it is in its first, fine, careless rapture, it has all too often degenerated into intellectual dishonesty, smugness, laziness and disregard of all promptings to reappraisal.

If Paul explicitly denied the Greek cult of wisdom and philosophy, he also implicitly denied the cult of beauty. In beauty, physical and spiritual, the Greeks felt that man came closest to the divine. In the words of the sixth-century BC poet Theognis, the Muses sang: 'What is lovely is beloved; what is not lovely is not beloved', and nowhere do we see this more clearly than in the Greek cult of the body. Watching the games on the isthmus of Corinth, the fifth-century BC poet Bacchylides sang of a young athlete:

In the five events he shone
As the brilliant moon of the mid-moth night
Makes the rays of the stars turn pale.
So in the boundless concourse of the Greeks
He showed off his wonderful body
As he hurled the round quoit.

(IX: 27-32)

This is an enthusiasm Paul did not share. It is true that Paul's remarks about the body have frequently been misunderstood. The Semites did not divide man into his body and soul; that is a Greek concept which they, and Paul with them, would not easily have understood. Man was a composite entity: body and soul formed an indissoluble whole. When Paul speaks, as he often does, in derogatory terms about the 'flesh' he is not referring to man's body as opposed to his spirit. In Paul, flesh means unredeemed man, man who has not been touched by the salvation brought about by the Cross. Later authors of the gentile world with Greek-trained intellects would see in Paul's denunciation of flesh a defamation of the body which he did not intend. For Paul, flesh (*sarx*) as opposed to the spirit (*pneuma*) did not indicate a dichotomy. Man's unredeemed body/soul would put off this corruption and become redeemed body/soul (*pneuma*) which would rise again whole and entire with Christ at the *parousia*.

Nevertheless Paul was not a friend to the body. He was beginning to grapple with the fact that Christ was a long time coming, and that some Christians had died before the *parousia* – what had happened to them? Would they also enjoy the benefits of salvation? Certainly they would, was his reply. Man was waiting and longing for the return of Christ and while he dwelt in the world he was exiled from his real home; the ultimate seal of that exile was his body, in which he lived in this world:

For us our homeland is in heaven and from heaven comes the saviour we are waiting for, the Lord Jesus Christ, and he will transfigure these wretched bodies of ours into copies of his glorious body.

(Philippians 3: 21)

In baptism the Christian has died with Christ; he is dead to the world and the world is dead to him. As long as he remains alive, imprisoned in the body, he is exiled from his real homeland. It is not a very good press for the body to call it 'wretched' or 'vile', even if for Paul it is only vile in so far as it falls short of the perfection that awaits it when it is most fully redeemed at death or at the *parousia*:

> To live in the body, then, means to be exiled from the Lord, going as we do by faith and not by sight, we are full of confidence I say and actually want to be exiled from the body and make our home with the Lord.
>
> (2 Corinthians 5: 6-7)

The Christian therefore learns to devalue the body as a second-best home, a temporary stop-over while he is waiting for the *parousia*.

There is no hint in Paul that the body can be a valuable aid to salvation. Quite the contrary – in his body man most clearly feels his 'unspiritual self', his most unredeemed self:

> So I find it to be a law that when I want to do right, evil lies close at hand. For I delight in the law of God in my inmost self, but I see in my members another law at war with the law of my mind and making me captive to the law of sin which dwells in my members. Wretched man that I am! who will deliver me from this body of death? Thanks be to God through Jesus Christ, our Lord! So then, I of myself serve the law of God with my mind, but with my body I serve the law of sin.
>
> (Romans 7: 21-25)

In this passage Paul is talking about unredeemed man in a state of original sin. But it also reads as though he is writing of the Christian who still feels the dregs of sin's slavery in himself. In passages like this, Paul has inadvertently bequeathed to Christians, because of his misunderstood use of the word 'flesh', a sense of connection, of cause and effect, between the body and sin. Admittedly, Paul elsewhere praises the body: 'Your body, you know, is holy; it is the Temple of the Holy Spirit' (1 Corinthians 6: 19); but this praise follows and justifies a command to abstain from sex: 'Keep away from fornication.' Man's body can lead him directly into sin, which for Paul is only a temporary state of affairs.

In Greece, Paul encountered the worship of the body that was symbolised by the cult of athletics. To Paul, however, the body of the Olympic athlete was not a revelation of beauty as it was for the Greeks, but a symbol of exiled man straining towards the world to come:

> Not that I have become perfect yet, I have not yet won the prize . . . All I can say is that I forget the past and I strain ahead for what is still to come; I am racing for the finish, for the prize to which God calls us upwards to receive in Christ Jesus.
>
> (Philippians 3: 12-15)

Later Christians used Paul as a basis for their own neuroses of celibacy, and the mistake is easy to understand. There is in Paul's rejection of the world and his slighting of the body a sense of isolation, the isolation of the exile who is not at home in his body. For Paul, marriage is not an expression of love so much as a means of legalising the sexual appetite for those unfortunate Christians who are not able to manage without it. It would be better to be like Paul himself, he maintains, celibate and waiting and straining for the *parousia*. Later Christians would outlaw marriage altogether; Paul's disciple Luke implies that any serious Christian would leave his wife to follow Christ (Luke 14: 26). Paul does not go to these lengths but he is grudging, at the least, about marriage and sex. 'If they cannot control their sexual urges, they should get married since it is better to be married than to be tortured' (1 Corinthians 7: 9).

Later many Christians followed Luke. Tertullian insisted on the renunciation of marriage, since it was based on the same act as harlotry. Jerome wrote that married people live 'like cattle' with one another and were no different from 'pigs and irrational animals'. Augustine made Paul's connection between the body and original sin. It was inherited physically, he maintained, by the embryo from his copulating parents. Through their misapprehension of Paul's thinking, these later theologians were, with Paul, responsible for a further schizophrenic element in Christianity. Nobody writes more movingly than Paul on love, on charity. Yet his grudging remarks about marriage herald the Christian divide between love and sex. Love is the supreme virtue for a Christian, but our bodies express the fact that we are not yet fully redeemed, hence the split between the sexual act and love itself. For Paul this strain would soon be eased at the *parousia*; but when strain is prolonged indefinitely it can become sickness.

There is an unhealthiness about the way erotic imagery is so frequently used by Christians to describe the union of Christ with the soul, when the reality of sex itself has been rejected. We see this most clearly in the third-century works of Origen, who in the introduction to his Commentary on the Song of Songs warned the reader not to read the book unless all his sexual desire had been eliminated. Origen himself so hated his own sexuality that he castrated himself.

While we are alive, we cannot live anywhere except in our own bodies. Our senses are our only messengers to the world around us and the only way we can receive the world. There is inevitably solitude involved in Paul's notion of sexual love and marriage as second best to the isolation of celibacy, just as there is solitude in the Christian feeling that the body and senses are 'wretched'. We turn away from a world with which we cannot trustingly communicate and are plunged into an isolation of introspection. Once there, we are no better off, since Paul has taught us that we cannot freely inhabit our own minds, which can teach us nothing of value. We are in exile, waiting for our Heavenly homeland.

Paul's sermon on the Areopagus has become famous. It has been seen as an example of good missionary methods; Paul has tailored his gospel to the Athenians' needs. However, the sermon is probably an invention of Luke's. It relies entirely on understanding Christ according to natural wisdom and philosophy, which Paul would not have countenanced. What Luke is doing, with customary New Testament freedom, is telling us what he, Luke, would have said if he had had a chance to preach at Athens. 'Men of Athens,' he has Paul begin:

> I have seen for myself how extremely scrupulous you are in all religious matters, because I noticed, as I strolled round admiring your sacred monuments, that you had an altar inscribed: To an Unknown God. Well, the God whom I proclaim is in fact the one whom you already worship without knowing it.

> (Acts 17: 22-23)

This is a very ingenious idea, but it is difficult to imagine Paul 'strolling' anywhere, let alone admiring idolatrous statues like a tourist. There follows a logical explanation of the falseness of idolatry, and Paul is made to speak of a God who is the source of life and in whom 'we live and move and have our being' (Acts 17: 26). This last famous phrase is a quotation from the poet Epimenedes of Knossos. Luke follows this up smartly by another quotation from the *Phainomena* of Aratus; Paul, he claims, was bending over backwards to preach his gospel to the Athenians in their own terms. These bland remarks about a God who can be discovered by natural reason by men of 'goodwill' bears no relation at all to Paul's gospel about a crucified Christ. Only in the last sentence of the sermon does Paul mention the resurrection of Jesus and then only in veiled terms.

Luke says the Athenians rejected out of hand the idea of the resurrection of a dead body, and in this he may be right. The idea of a physical resurrection would have been discarded as fanciful and barbarous nonsense by both the Stoics and the Epicureans, the two major philosophical schools of the time. For both, death was the end of at least one existence, possibly the end of everything; it was certainly a farewell to everything man had ever known, rather than a physical continuation of it. Whatever the reason, Paul was entirely unsuccessful in Athens, and we have no record of any church founded here. But if Athens rejected Paul, Paul also rejected Athens and all that it represented in the name of human development and culture. At Athens, symbolically, Paul turned Christianity against the empirical world.

This was understandable. For Paul the world was finished anyway. 'The world as we know it is passing away', he would write later (1 Corinthians 7: 21). But two thousand years later the world is still very much with us. Paul's spiritual sense of exile from the Judaism that continually rejected him, his constant travelling, a perpetual foreigner offended by the pagan world around him, and his belief in the imminence of the *parousia*, constituted a threefold sense of exile that Christianity still bears today; alongside this developed the notion of the makeshift quality of man's inhabitation of a physical body, which Paul compared to a tent that the traveller sleeps in temporarily and folds up in the morning:

> For we know that when the tent that we live in on earth is folded up, there is a house built by God for us, an everlasting home not made with human hands, in the heavens. In this

present state, it is true, we groan as we wait with longing to put on our heavenly home over the other; we should like to be found wearing clothes and not without them. Yes, we groan and find it a burden being still in this tent, not that we want to strip it off, but to put the second garment over it and to have what must die taken up into life. This is the purpose for which God made us, and he has given us the pledge of the spirit.

We are always full of confidence, then, when we remember that to live in the body means to be exiled from the Lord.

(2 Corinthians 5: 1-6)

Paul is longing for this present existence to be over, for the *parousia* to come before he has died. Later Christians took up this theme from Paul. Life in the world can be of no interest to the Christian, whose real home is 'in the heavens'. Like a true exile, man can only 'groan' over the discomforts of his makeshift, nomadic existence, yearning for the future.

One of the first of Paul's disciples to pick up this theme was the author of the Epistle to the Hebrews, a converted Jew. He writes of the Jewish patriarchs, starting with Abraham, who followed God's call with such faith that he left his home in Ur and journeyed to the promised land with no guarantee beyond his hope in God.

By faith he arrived, *as a foreigner*,[1] in the promised land and lived there as if in a strange country, with Isaac and Jacob, who were heirs with him of the same promise. They lived in tents, while he looked forward to a city founded and designed by God . . .

All these died in faith, before receiving any of the things that had been promised, but they saw them in the far distance and welcomed them, recognising that they were only *strangers and nomads on earth*.[2] People who use such terms about themselves make it quite clear that they are in search of their

1. Genesis 23: 4; 26: 3; 35: 12.
2. Genesis 23: 4.

real homeland. They can hardly have meant the country they came from, since they had the opportunity to go back to it, but in fact they were longing for a better homeland, their heavenly homeland.

(Hebrews 11: 8-10, 13-16)

It is the same for the Christian, the author insists. 'In this life we have no abiding city, but we look for one in the life to come' (Hebrews 13: 14).

Most thinking people feel out of tune with the world from time to time. The seductive force of an ideal that justifies this sense that we are made for something better makes us respond enthusiastically to this aspect of Christianity. To despise the world in knowledge of future fulfilment will make us invulnerable to the shocks of time and chance. 'I have despised the kingdom of the world and all worldly attractions,' sings the novice on the day he makes his vows in a covent or monastery, 'for the sake of my Lord Jesus Christ, whom I have seen, whom I have loved, in whom I have believed, in whom I have delighted'.

Yet not just monks despise the world and retreat from it. To reject the world is an ideal that has been placed before all Christians by devotional writers through the ages, such as the extremely influential Thomas à Kempis, author of *The Imitation of Christ*. He was a monk, writing for monks, but his book has been a favourite with laymen also, and not only with Roman Catholics. George Eliot's Maggie Tulliver in *The Mill on the Floss* finds in it a source of inspiration and destructive consolation. 'Renounce the world' runs through the book like an insistent beat:

If you would taste true pleasure and receive the fullness of My consolation, know this: that in the despising of worldly things and the shunning of base delights shall be your blessing and you shall win abundant consolation. The more you withdraw yourself from the comfort of creatures, the sweeter and more potent will be the consolations that you will find in Me. But you will not find these at once, or without sorrow, toil and effort. Old habits will stand in your way, but by better they will be overcome. The body will complain, but by fervour of the spirit it can be disciplined.

(*The Imitation of Christ* 3, 12)

The body is a hindrance to the spiritual man and must be disciplined and quelled. Nor is the mind a refuge or help for the retreating soul. The author advises us at the beginning of his book to 'restrain an inordinate desire for knowledge, in which is found much anxiety and deception'. Later he says:

At the Day of Judgement, we shall not be asked what we have read, but what we have done; not how eloquently we have spoken, but how holily we have lived. Tell me, where are now all those Masters and Doctors whom you knew so well in their lifetime in the full flower of their learning? Other men now sit in their seats, and they are hardly ever called to mind. In their lifetime they seemed of great account, but now no one speaks of them.

Oh, how swiftly the glory of the world passes away! If only the lives of these men had been as admirable as their learning.

(*The Imitation of Christ* 1, 3)

If *The Imitation of Christ* has been popular that is because it has brilliantly expressed this Christian mood. We cannot reach outward to the world, we can only retreat to an inner solitude of spirit:

Enter into your room, and shut out the clamour of the world, as it is written, *Commune with your own heart, and in your chamber, and be still.*[1] Within your cell you will discover what you will only too often lose abroad.

(*The Imitation of Christ* 1, 20)

1. Psalms 4: 4.

The Christian cannot allow himself to commune with the world but only with God. Augustine, that great Paulinist, caught this spirit perfectly when he addressed his *Confessions* directly to God and not to the world which would actually read them.

The paradox is that, as Christianity would have it, 'God so loved the world' that he sent it his own son (John 3: 16). Christianity teaches the doctrine of the incarnation, that God himself, the second person of the blessed Trinity, descended from Heaven into a virgin's womb and became flesh. God took a human body and a human mind, entered our world and used it to redeem itself. If God so loved the world why should we despise it? And if God took a body and a mind, surely these have been made valuable because God valued them so much? If God so loved humanity, can we say with Paul that 'there is nothing to boast about in anything human' (1 Corinthians 3: 22)? How can Paul have thought such a thing?

The answer is that Paul did not believe in the incarnation. As a Jew his monotheism was far too strong. He had never heard of the Holy Trinity in our sense, even though he speaks of the Father, the Son and the Spirit. We have seen that Jesus never claimed to be God; that when he said he was the Son of God he would have meant only that he was very close to God. In the synoptic gospels, those of Matthew, Mark and Luke, there is no evidence that Jesus claimed to be God, nor that any of these evangelists thought he was. This has long been accepted by many scholars. When the angel Gabriel announced the birth of Jesus to Mary, it was well within a long tradition of miraculous Biblical births. We need only think of Sarah whose conception was also announced by a divine messenger and who, albeit no virgin, was long past the menopause. Her giving birth was just as miraculous as the birth of Jesus, yet no one ever thought that Issac was God. Paul didn't know the story of the annunciation, because Luke wrote his gospel some twenty years after Paul's death. Paul speaks of Christ having been 'born of a woman'; he never mentions Mary's virginity, which, given his views on sex and on women, he certainly would have done if he had had the chance. Paul thought that when Jesus was alive on earth and 'in the flesh' he was born in the normal way and was an ordinary human being. When Paul speaks of Jesus being 'divine' and 'equal to God' (Philippians 2: 6) he does not mean that Jesus was the second person of the blessed Trinity, any more than a Jew did when he called the Messiah the 'Son of God'. Paul means that Jesus was always a special individual, close to God. This early Christian hymn speaks of Jesus as though he were pre-existing in some way, with God, before he descended to earth:

> His state was divine, yet he did not cling to his equality with God but emptied himself to assume the condition of a slave, and became as men are.
>
> (Philippians 2: 6-7)

In Judaism there had been a well-established tradition for specially favoured individuals to have dwelt with God before they descended to earth. Some of the rabbis said that the Messiah was now living with God before he came to redeem Israel. Others said that the Torah had dwelt with God as a favoured being, before descending to earth on Mount Sinai. The late Old Testament concept of a personified Wisdom has the same Idea:

> She is a breath of the power of God, pure emanation of the glory of the Almighty; hence nothing impure can find a way into her. She is a reflection of the eternal light, untarnished mirror of God's active power, image of his goodness.
>
> (Wisdom 7: 25-26)

Solomon is made to pray for this wisdom of Yahweh to descend to earth:

> With you is wisdom, she who knows your works, she who was present when you made the world; she understands what is pleasing in your eyes and what agrees with your commandments. Dispatch her from the holy heavens, send her forth from your throne of glory to help me and to toil with me and teach me what is pleasing to you.

(Wisdom 9: 9-10)

Neither Isaac nor Wisdom is considered to be God. The Jewish writers' monotheism was too strong for any such claim, however exalted these creatures may be. Likewise Paul was unable to make any such assertion for Jesus.

The doctrine of the incarnation is late arriving on the scene. We do not find it until we turn to the Gospel According to St John, written in about AD 100, some seventy years after Jesus' death and about fifty years after Paul was writing his Epistles. In John, 'the Word was made flesh and dwelt amongst us' (1: 14). In John Jesus makes claims that can truly said to be divine, as he does not do in the synoptics. At last the phrase 'Son of God' is beginning to have non-Jewish and trinitarian overtones when Jesus says, for example, 'I and the Father are one' (John 10: 30).

If Paul believed that Jesus, while on earth, was an ordinary man, he also believed Jesus had in some sense been 'promoted' by his resurrection to an exalted status. This Matthew, Mark and Luke also believed. After the resurrection, Jesus, they say, appeared to his apostles as an apotheosised human being. He had been lifted to a transcendent state, but he was still an individual man, however glorious and full of the power of God. He had blazed a trail for mankind to follow in his flesh, and one day we would be as he is. The accounts of these resurrection appearances are different from Paul's account, as we have seen. For him the apparitions of Jesus to the apostles were 'visions' no different from his own:

> The news is about the Son of God who, according to the human nature he took, was a descendant of David: it is about Jesus Christ our Lord who in the order of the Spirit, the spirit of holiness that was in him, was proclaimed Son of God in all his power through his resurrection from the dead.
>
> (Romans 1: 3-5)

Jesus was the Son of God by virtue of his resurrection, and Christians are 'sons' too by adoption. Jesus has, as the Kyrios, a specially exalted status: after Christ had lived a humble life and died on the cross:

> God raised him high and gave him the name which is above all other names so that all beings in the heavens, on earth and in the underworld should bend the knee at the name of Jesus and that every tongue should acclaim Jesus Christ as Lord to the glory of God the Father.
>
> (Philippians 2: 9-11)

Notice that it is God who raised up Jesus from the dead in Paul, and whenever he speaks about Jesus, the Kyrios Christos, and the Father, there is always a distinction, albeit a very fine one, between the two. If Jesus has been glorified by becoming the Lord it is for the glory of God the Father. Even after the resurrection Paul's monotheism was too strong for him to say, as John would, that Jesus and his Father were one.

The irony is that Paul, who did not believe in the incarnation, gave Christianity its jaundiced mood about humanity. The author of the First Letter of St John gives us some indication of what incarnational theology could mean for the body and the humanity of man:

> Something which has existed since the beginning, that we have heard, and we have seen with our own eyes; that we

have watched and touched with our hands: the Word, who is
life – this is our subject. That Life was made visible.

(1 John 1: 1)

Here the senses of man are engaged in the discovery of God.
Man is reaching out to touch and see the tangible and visible
revelation in Jesus Christ, the Word made flesh. But alas by
this time the tribulations that the Christians were beginning
to endure in the world – from the Jews, who had ejected
them from the synagogues, and later, from the Roman
authorities – has even here reinforced Paul's original insight
that the world and Christianity cannot love one another:

> You must not love this passing world or anything that is in
> the world. The love of the Father cannot be in any man who
> loves the world, because nothing the world has to offer – the
> sensual body, the lustful eye, pride in possessions – could
> ever come from the Father, but only from the world; and the
> world with all it craves for is coming to an end.
>
> (1 John 2: 15-17)

At the same time as Paul's efficient missionary methods
were laying a foundation for a Church firmly embedded in
the world, a Church established alongside the strongholds
of the Roman Empire, he was, with typical Pauline paradox,
beginning the tendency which would separate Christianity
from the world. The later doctrine of the incarnation, which
logically should have contradicted this tendency, did nothing to mitigate the melancholy sense of exile. No one has
caught the Christian mood of loneliness more perfectly than
the great Paulinist, St Augustine. Here he mistakenly uses
Paul's image of flesh to describe the Pauline state of exile:

> Every man is a foreigner in this life; in which life ye see that
> with flesh we are covered round, through which flesh the
> heart cannot be seen . . . in this sojourning of fleshly life
> everyone carrieth his own heart and every heart to every
> other heart is shut.
>
> (*Expositians on the Book of Psalms*, Commentary on Psalm 55)

5 Christian authority

After his unsuccessful visit to Athens, Paul went to Corinth in about AD 52. There he founded a lively church but a contentious one. Where modern Christian leaders frequently have to struggle against the apathy of their flocks, Paul's problem in Corinth was different. His converts there were hyperactive, and in his efforts to pull them back to his own gospel we see another side of Paul emerging: Paul the visionary now had to start controlling the visions of others. Paul the individualist, who had felt entirely confident about taking off on his own after his conversion, without any discussions with more experienced Christians, now insisted that other individualists obey his gospel. Paul, who had rebelled against the 'pillars' of the Jerusalem church, now encountered rebellion among his own converts. In order to protect his gospel, Paul became increasingly authoritarian and so laid a pattern for future Christian authoritarianism.

Corinth, the capital of Achaia, was a good place to establish a missionary centre. It had been completely destroyed in the third Punic War, but rebuilt by Caesar. It was a modern city, predominantly Roman in style and concept, and like Thessalonika the seat of a proconsul. If these Roman links would have pleased Paul, it is probable that other aspects of Corinth did little to endear him further to it. It was a wealthy commercial city with a reputation for immorality. While the merchants who poured into Corinth's two harbours and the visitors who came for miles to the famous isthmus games would have made Corinth an ideal centre for the spreading of the gospel, Paul was probably appalled by the luxury of the city and the immorality of its residents. His converts were mostly from the poorer and uneducated classes, as he reminds them in his letter.

Paul stayed in Corinth initially for about eighteen months, and all went relatively smoothly at first. He lived with two Roman Jews, Aquila and Prisca, working alongside them as a tent-maker. Aquila and Prisca had been expelled from Rome by Claudius' edict and perhaps they told Paul about the establishment of a church there. We know from the Epistles that this couple became loyal disciples of Paul, and when he left Corinth for Ephesus they accompanied him there. From Acts of the Apostles, one might imagine that all was sweetness and light within the Corinthian community, but Paul's two great letters to the Corinthians show that Luke has been doing his usual cover-up job. He admits that Paul had trouble with the Jews and was ejected from the synagogue, having to move to the house of a Godfearer called Justus. Paul's converts were mostly gentiles, but also, Luke says, there were some Jewish converts, including the leader of the synagogue and his family. Luke omits entirely, however, the disputes that sprang up in Corinth within the church itself.

It is usually thought that Christians in the early Church were strongly united in faith and purpose, but we have already seen that this was far from the case. There were many different brands of Christianity, some of them antagonistic to each other. Even beneath the placid surface of Luke's narrative we can glimpse these divisions, and Paul's letters show how disruptive they could be. In Corinth there was a group of Jewish Christians who owed allegiance to Peter, or Cephas. After Paul left the city to go to Ephesus,

Apollos, a Jew from Alexandria, arrived. Luke writes a revealing sentence about him: 'He was an eloquent man, with a sound knowledge of the scriptures, and yet, though he had been given instruction in the Way of the Lord and preached with great spiritual earnestness and was accurate in all the details he taught about Jesus, he had only experienced the baptism of John' (Acts 18: 24-25). What kind of Christianity can this have been? How was it possible to be accurate about Jesus if you did not progress further than the baptism of John the Baptist. When Paul went on to Ephesus, whence Apollos had come, he presumably found a number of disciples evangelised by Apollos. Yet even of this we cannot be certain:

> When he asked, 'Did you receive the Holy Spirit when you became believers?' they answered, 'No, we were never even told that there was such a thing as the Holy Spirit.' 'Then how were you baptised?' he asked. 'With John's baptism,' they replied. 'John's baptism,' said Paul, 'was a baptism of repentance; but he insisted that the people should believe in the one who was to come after him – in other words, Jesus.' When they heard this they were baptised in the name of the Lord Jesus, and the moment Paul laid his hands on them, the Holy Spirit came down on them, and they began to speak with tongues and to prophesy. There were about twelve of these men.
>
> (Acts 19: 1-7)

We know so little about the belief and different groupings in the early Church. Apollos came from Alexandria, which would later become an important church, but we know nothing about its foundation. Nor do we know about the foundation of the Roman church. We don't know how the Jewish Christians of the diaspora differed, if they differed at all, from the Judaic *minim*. In Corinth, Paul's converts had to contend with other people who believed in Jesus but who believed a lot of different things about him. From his letters to the Corinthians we learn about another sect, who have been dubbed the Enthusiasts by scholars because of their emphasis on the inspiration of the spirit and spiritual freedom. Given the fact that the early Christians were dependent entirely on oral communication, it is hardly surprising that the gospel quickly changed from one locality, and from one preacher, to another. Sometimes these contrasting emphases would be slight, sometimes they would concern such vital doctrines as the conversion of gentiles, baptism, and the holy spirit.

Of the myriad brands of Christianity that existed in the first century the one that became official was the theology of Paul. The other types of Christianity were suppressed and fell into oblivion. We know about some of these rival types of Christianity in fragmentary form only because they make incidental appearances in the letters of Paul, or because they are included by the Pauline Luke in his narrative. There were perhaps many more Christianities about which we know nothing whatever. How did Paul manage to impose his view of Christianity on succeeding generations of Christians? Partly it is because of his efficient missionary policy, partly because of his intellectual ability in constructing for Christianity a coherent theology. Partly it may spring from his vehemence and authority in imposing his gospel on his converts to the exclusion of others.

The Jews tried to take action about Paul's teaching and brought him before the proconsul, Gallio, who was in Corinth from AD 52, as we know from an inscription at Delphi. Gallio refused to take sides in the matter, because the nature of the Jewish complaint was an entirely religious one: 'If it is only quibbles about words and names, and about your own Law, then you must deal with it yourselves – I have no intention at all of making legal decisions about things like that' (Acts 18: 15). We know that Luke is pro-Roman in his account, but if he is correct here we see

Paul being assisted and protected by Roman law, in a way that Jesus could have been if his offence was simply religious.

Later the positions would be reversed and Christianity would be able to support the empire. When Constantine saw his vision of the Cross in the sky, causing him to make Christianity the state religion, it is more likely that the vision he had was not Paul's vision of Christ crucified but Paul's administrative and political vision of a Church grouped round the centres of Roman administration. In Christianity, Constantine saw a means of uniting his unwieldy empire. He was not an informed Christian; on the contrary, he was not baptised until he was on his death bed and then he was baptised by a member of the Arian heresy. However, in Christianity he could see a politically cohesive force.

The trouble in Corinth began after Paul had left the city. A series of Enthusiast preachers began to deliver a gospel which was quite opposed to Paul's. As far as we can tell from his letters they believed that they had already risen from the dead with Christ; they would never die and were therefore already perfect. Where Paul believed the Christian life was a way of death, Christ's death, the Enthusaists believed they were already enjoying the glorified life. Where Paul believed the Christian was in exile in this world, straining forward to future glorification, the Enthusiasts made themselves very much at home in immoral Corinth. They were already saved, fully redeemed, nothing could harm them; they could take part in idolatrous meals and sleep with prostitutes.

These preachers believed that they were directly inspired by the spirit and competed in charisma. At church services, people broke out into 'spiritual' tongues that nobody else could understand; they leapt up to prophesy or to teach, shouting one another down and vying with one another to get a yell in edgeways. Spectacular miracles were performed. And because each Christian was inspired directly by the spirit, each Christian was a law unto himself. Chaos was near, and Christian unity within the community at Corinth was seriously threatened.

Paul himself was a charismatic. He too had visions, spoke in tongues, had mystical experiences, worked miracles. When he defends himself against the 'arch-apostles' as he calls them, who seem to have been denigrating Paul's authority by boasting about their greater charismatic prowess, he writes ironically:

> Though I am a nobody, there is not a thing these arch-apostles have that I do not have as well. You have seen done among you all the things that mark the true apostle, unfailingly produced: the signs, the marvels the miracles. Is there anything of which you have had less than the other churches have had, except that I have not myself been a burden on you!
>
> (2 Corinthians, 12: 12-13)

In Corinth he could see the danger of these individualistic spiritual gifts. Paul insisted that such gifts must be for the sake of the whole community. There was no point in speaking in tongues if nobody else could understand them. What benefit would that be to the Church?

> If your tongue does not produce intelligible speech, how can anyone know what you are saying? You will be talking to the air. There are any number of different languages in the world, and not one of them is meaningless, but if I am ignorant of what the sounds mean, I am a savage to the man who is speaking, and he is a savage to me. It is the same in your own case: since you aspire to spiritual gifts, concentrate on those which will grow to benefit the community.
>
> (1 Corinthians 14: 9-12)

This is not sour grapes. Paul's attitude towards them is both self-assertive and responsible:

> I thank God, that I have a greater gift of tongues than all of you, but when I am in the presence of the community, I would rather say five words that mean something than ten thousand words in a tongue. Brothers, you are not to be childish in your outlook.
>
> (1 Corinthians 14: 18-20)

No one part of the Church was any more important than the others. Like the limbs of the body, they were all indispensable, each part with its separate but vital functions. All Christians were 'in Christ'.

Paul opposed the Enthusiasts strongly in the surviving letters he wrote to the troubled Corinthian church; some of the letters, it seems, did not survive. He made another visit to Corinth and on a further occasion sent a personal envoy – the messenger's authority was deliberately flouted. Like the pagan apostles he had encountered in Thessalonika the 'arch-apostles' of Corinth used vulgar, worldly methods to enforce their message. They complained that Paul was a poor speaker; he did not make use of rhetoric or eloquence. Paul addresses himself to their objections:

> I do not want you to think of me as someone who only frightens you by letter. Someone said, 'He writes powerfully and strongly-worded letters but when he is with you you see only half a man and no preacher at all.'
>
> (2 Corintians 10: 10)

It also seems that the Enthusiast apostles were getting the Corinthians to keep them in food and money and otherwise behaving disgracefully:

> When I was with you and ran out of money, I was no burden to anyone; the brothers who came from Macedonia provided me with everything I wanted. I was very careful, and I always

shall be, not to be a burden to you in any way, and by
Christ's truth in me, this cause of boasting will never be
taken from me in the regions of Achaia. Would I do that if I
did not love you? God knows I do. I intend to go on doing
what I am doing now . . .

So many others have been boasting about their worldly
achievements that I will boast about myself. You are all wise
men who can cheerfully tolerate fools, yes, even to tolerating
someone who makes slaves of you, makes you feed him,
imposes on you, orders you about and slaps you in the face.

(2 Corinthians 11: 9-13, 18-20)

As each individual Christian believed that he was divinely
inspired and that he had the answer, how was anyone to
know who was right? Paul's answer was quite simple. He
was.

It is natural that he should have taken such an attitude.
He had been a Christian for years, was almost one of the
founder members, and these 'arch-apostles' were newcomers. He knew more than they did: 'I may not be a
polished speaker,' he writes, 'but as for knowledge, that is
a different matter' (2 Corinthians 11: 6). Paul's travels and
long missionary experience throughout the empire had
given him a wider perspective than these Corinthians
bounded by petty local views possessed. Paul also claims
that the true apostle is the one who suffers the most; he had
worked harder for the gospel than almost anyone else,
while these 'arch-apostles' were idly waiting around for the
parousia. Furthermore, and this Paul does not tell the
Corinthians, he was an extremely clever man and had an
academic training, whether or not he had studied under
Gamaliel; he argues and uses scripture just like a learned
rabbi. The Corinthians, on the other hand, as he gently
reminds them, were not learned. They were simple people:
'At the time when you were called, how many of you were
wise in the ordinary sense of the word, how many were

influential or came from noble families?' (1 Corinthians 1: 26).

Paul never doubted the authenticity of his vision and mission. And not only in Corinth did he have to exercise his authority over his converts. We have seen that in Galatia he had to contend with Judaising Christians; there was a good deal of opposition to him at Ephesus, though we cannot be sure of its nature. When Paul arrived in Athens, he heard about the persecution of the Christians in Thessalonika and had instantly to send Timothy back to bring him news. Timothy came with questions about those who had already died before the *parousia* – would they enjoy the salvation of Jesus, when would the last day occur? Besides the Enthusiasts, Christians at Corinth had asked questions about marriage and celibacy, about the Eucharist, about mixing with the pagan world. All these questions urgently needed answers. Paul's brilliance enabled him to see these practical questions in the context of a rational and intellectual scheme. He was not content to give a quick *ad hoc* answer, but always related it to the Christian message as a whole, while firmly asserting his right to do so. Sometimes he makes it clear that he is handing on a tradition, sometimes he will speak on his own initiative, as he does on the celibacy issue: 'I have no directions from the Lord but give my own opinion.' (1 Corinthians 7: 25). Sometimes he simply issues a directive to all the churches. Unlike his successors, Paul was writing in the midst of conflict – in whichever church he happened to be in at the time, on the road, in prison, on the run, in sickness and exhaustion. Always it was a time of crisis. There is no systematic development of Paul's thought, but there is coherence. What he did for Christianity was to give it an intellectual structure. Just as he systematised his visions into efficient policy, so too he made a rational and logical framework out of the essential irrationality of faith and vision.

The coherence of Paul's thought gives it its power, and the power of his authority made it impossible to overlook his theology. 'I am an apostle,' he writes simply 'and I have seen Jesus our Lord' (1 Corinthians 9: 1). Sometimes, though, we wince at the vehemence of his claims; he threatens and bullies when necessary: 'It is for you to decide, do I come with a stick in my hand or in the spirit of love and goodwill?' (1 Corinthians 3: 21).

> This will be the third time I have to come to you . . . I gave warning when I was with you the second time and I give warning now, too, before I come, to those who sinned before and to any others, that when I come again, I shall have no mercy.
>
> (2 Corinthians 13: 1-2)

Sometimes he seems to be deliberately holding himself back from wrath: 'That is why I am writing this from a distance, so that when I am with you I shall not need to be strict, with the authority that the Lord gave me for building up and not for destroying' (2 Corinthians 13: 10). On all sides Paul was struggling with persecution, stupidity, ignorance, arrogance and genuine mistakes. Nevertheless, with the later history of Christianity in mind, we sometimes feel a premonitory shudder when we listen to Paul enforcing his gospel above everybody else's:

> From Paul to the churches of Galatia, and from all the brothers who are here with me, an apostle who does not owe his authority to men or his appointment to any human being but who has been appointed by Jesus Christ and by God the Father who raised Jesus from the dead . . .
>
> I am astonished at the promptness with which you have turned away from the one who called you and have decided to follow a different version of the Good News. Not that there can be more than one Good News; it is merely that some trouble-makers among you want to change the Good News of Christ; and let me warn you that if anyone preaches

a version of the Good News different from the one we have
already preached to you, whether it be ourselves or an angel
of heaven, he is to be *anathema*.

(Galatians 1: 1-2, 6-8)

Paul's faith, like that of Abraham, was the faith of Judaism,
whose God was too transcendent and mysterious to be tied
down by any one man's definition. Paul's faith meant being
prepared to follow Christ into the uncertainties of the world
of the spirit. Yet, as Paul insists on the supremacy of his own
gospel, another disturbing element in the concept of faith
begins to emerge. Paul's insistence that his converts believe
exactly what he believes has set a sad example to later
Christians. 'Believe what I believe or you are anathema' is a
cry that has resounded through Christian history in its
appalling record of heartless and arrogant inquisition and
persecution. Christianity has learned from those who have
persecuted it how to persecute its own deviants. The papacy
is one example of its autocratic power, controlling rigidly
the belief of its subjects on pain of damnation. If you want to
be saved you must believe every article of Catholic faith,
where it be an essential matter or not. Nearly every sect can
point to a similar intolerance, to bigotry, to bloody persecution. And for all this, though he would have been horrified
to see it, Paul had set the precedent.

There is a dichotomy in the way that Christians view and
practise authority. In St John's gospel, before the Passion,
Jesus, the Master, washes like a servant the feet of his
disciples. 'If I, then, the Lord and Master, have washed your
feet, you should wash each other's feet' (John 13: 14). Luke
and the synoptics recall these words of Jesus:

> A dispute arose also among them about which should be
> reckoned the greatest, but he said to them, 'Among the
> Pagans it is the kings who lord it over them and those who
> have the authority over them are given the title Benefactor.
> This must not happen with you. No; the greatest among you

must behave as if he were the youngest, the leader as if he were the one who serves. For who is the greater, the one at table or the one who serves? The one at table, surely. Yet here I am among you as one who serves.'

(Luke 22: 24-27)

Instead of emulating Jesus here, Christian rulers have frequently exercised Paul's ruthless authority, rather than the humble authority that Jesus recommends. In the gospels, Jesus is portrayed as a religious rebel, who inveighs against the establishment figures of Judaism. The distorted gospel portrait of the Pharisees ironically reminds us of many Christian leaders, past and present, of many denominations. Complacent and sure of their monopoly of truth, insisting on a sterile conformity with long-established practice, the libellous view of the Pharisees is, sadly, far too familiar from Christian examples. The Pharisees of the gospels have served as a model for Christian authoritarians far more than did Jesus himself – surely the point Pasolini was making in his film *The Gospel According to St Matthew*.

In Corinth, Paul insisted that greater than all the Enthusiasts' charismatic gifts was the virtue of charity, and it was to the Corinthians that he wrote his great hymn of charity or love:

Love is always patient and kind; it is never jealous. Love is never boastful or conceited; it is never rude or selfish; it does not take offence, and is not resentful. Love takes no pleasure in other peoples' sins and delights in truth; it is always ready to excuse, to trust, to hope, to endure whatever comes.

(1 Corinthians 13: 4-7)

Reading Paul's praise of charity, we may find ourselves raising our eyebrows: 'Love is always patient . . . never boastful or conceited . . . does not take offence . . . always ready to excuse.' This does not sound much like Paul who is often impatient with his rebellious converts, does boast about his gifts and sufferings when driven to it, does take offence. He writes bitterly to the Corinthians of the tears he has shed over their disputes and the attacks he has endured. Often he imputes the meanest motives to his opponents, and we may wonder about those 'arch-apostles' in Corinth. Were they really as bad as Paul depicts them? Or were the Judaisers in Galatia really as lacking in integrity as he says?

> It is only self-interest that makes them want to force circumcision on you – they want to escape persecution for the cross of Christ – they accept circumcision but do not keep the Law themselves – they only want you to be circumcised so that they can boast of the fact.
>
> (Galatians 6: 22-23)

We have only Paul's word for this. Is it not possible that some of the Judaisers may have been sincere? Paul does not piously turn the other cheek; he hits back hard.

The Sermon on the Mount had not been written when Paul wrote Galatians, and the 'Christian character' had not been fully defined. Paul's praise of charity is one of the first sketches of Christian virtue that we possess. Paul does not often sound like a canonised saint, and there is something refreshing about him. He does not hide his own pain under a reserved show of indifference, he does not take refuge in a forgiveness that is so detached from the world and fearful of feeling that it is sometimes difficult to understand what Christians mean by love. The ideal of Christian detachment from the world can lead to coldness and inhumanity. Thérèse of Lisieux writes of her fortune in avoiding the 'poison' of human friendship, in a way that is familiar from a reading of the lives of the canonised saints:

> I had a sensitive and affectionate nature, and I might easily have squandered my affections on other people . . . Lucky for me that I had so little gift of making myself agreeable; it has preserved me from grave dangers. I shall always be

grateful to our Lord for turning earthly friendships into bitterness for me, because, with a nature like mine, I could so easily have fallen into a snare . . . I don't see how it is possible for a heart given over to such earthly affections to attain any intimate union with God. I can't speak from experience because this immoderate love of creatures is a poison-draught which has always been kept away from my lips.

(*Autobiography of a Saint*, trans. Ronald Knox, 1: 13)

In some religious orders until recently friendship was regarded as a danger to the religious' love of God. Attitudes like that of Thérèse have been held up for admiration even to lay people. An underlying conviction of the 'danger' and 'snare' of human love, and of the impossibility of loving God and people at the same time, can lead to a Christian 'charity' that is little more than a hearty and heartless *bonhomie*.

Paul love his converts. Unlike the saints who would come after him, he loved them enough to be hurt by them, to be vulnerable to them, to be involved. He was immensely heartened, for example, when he heard from Titus how sorry the Corinthians were that they had hurt him, and he wrote to tell them so at once. Many later Christians who were striving for sanctity would probably regard such sensitivity as weak-minded. Paul is giving in to his affectionate nature. He does not regard his attachment to his converts as limiting his love of God. His tears over the defection of his converts and delight over their return would in many later Christian circles have been regarded as a woeful lack of detachment on his part, the implication being that Paul should be delighted to endure suffering for Christ and should beware of the dangers of human friendship. Paul transcends the repressions involved in too much charity. An ideal in which human warmth and involvement are sacrificed in the interests of detachment from all worldly things must result in strain and unnatural sublimation.

Thérèse of Lisieux's autobiography is a witness to the unhealthiness of this attitude; we read without surprise of her endless storms of tears, her tendency to psychosomatic illness and her neurotic sensitivity.

One of the letters where we see Paul's charity most tenderly is the Epistle to Philemon. Philemon's slave, Onesimus, has run away to Paul and Paul sends him back, punning gently on his name (*onesimus* means 'useful'):

> He was of no use to you before, but he will be useful now, as he has been to me. I am sending him back to you and with him – I could say – part of myself. I should have liked to keep him with me – he could have been a substitute for you, to help me while I am in the chains that the Good News has brought me . . . I know you have been deprived of Onesimus for a time, but it was only so you could have had him back for ever, not as a slave any more but as something better than a slave, a dear brother; especially dear to me, but how much dearer to you, as a blood-brother as well as a brother in the Lord.
>
> (Philemon 11-17)

If Paul's tenderness here has been praised, his sending Onesimus back to Philemon has been roundly censured. Supporting the Roman authorities is all very well, but supporting the appalling institution of slavery is another matter, it has been said. For generations Christians have followed Paul and have urged the poor and the exploited to put up with their lot; religion has indeed become 'the opium of the people'. This is all true, except that for Paul the imminence of the *parousia* meant that social reform was unnecessary. Also, however, Paul's insistence that Onesimus is now Philemon's brother is a radical statement. It was fundamental to Paul's theology that in Christ there were no divisions of race or class; in Christ there was neither Jew nor gentile, slave nor free. This principle was behind Paul's attitude over the circumcision controversy.

The troubles in Corinth reveal that Paul, against his better theological judgement, did think that in the kingdom of Christ there were second-class citizens – women:

> . . . what I want you to understand is that Christ is the head of every man, man is the head of woman and God is the head of Christ. For a man to pray or prophesy with his head covered is a sign of disrespect to his head. For a woman, however, it is a sign of disrespect to her head if she prays or prophesies unveiled; she might as well have her hair shaved off. In fact a woman who will not wear a veil ought to have her hair cut off. If a woman is ashamed to have her hair cut off or shaved, she ought to wear a veil.

> (1 Corinthians 11: 1-6)

Clearly in Corinth, among the other dissentient groups the women were taken advantage of the new freedom, speaking out in services and refusing to wear their veils. Considering the magnitude of the other disorders Paul is combating in this Epistle – incest; Enthusiasts resorting to prostitutes and eating at idolatrous meals; Christians suing one another in pagan courts; disorders at the Eucharist; theological factions and church divisions – the fact that the women are not wearing their veils seems an anti-climax. But for Paul, as can be seen by the vigour with which he attacks the problem, it was not a trivial matter at all. Women were getting out of line and forgetting their place as man's inferior.

> A man should certainly not cover his head, since he is the image of God and reflects God's glory. For man did not come from woman; no, woman came from man; and man was not created for the sake of woman, but woman was created for the sake of man. That is the argument for women's covering their heads with a symbol of the authority over them, out of respect for the angels.

> (1 Corinthians 11: 7-10)

Writing on the circumcision issue, Paul says that 'in Christ there are no more distinctions between Jew or Gentile, slave or free, male or female' (Galatians 3: 28). Christ had destroyed these old barriers and all were equal members of the body of Christ. Yet to the Corinthians he insists on women's inferior status. In the Christian meetings women are to remain silent, they 'must keep in the background. If they have any questions to ask, they should ask their husbands at home. It does not seem right for woman to raise her voice at meetings' (1 Corinthians 14: 35).

In Paul's defence, it might be said that this attitude appears only in the first letter to the Corinthians and that Luke mentions that women were of the greatest help to Paul on his travels and in the churches; for example Lydia, the seller of purples at Philippi. When he sends messages to individual Christians he does not relegate all the women to the end of the list, as a real woman-hater might have done; on the contrary, he distributes epithets like 'dear' or 'beloved' fairly between the women as much as the men. When he sends his regards to Aquila and Prisca he mentions Prisca first. It might be argued that Paul was only voicing the attitudes of Judaism, which was and has remained a male dominated religion. Such Judaic attitudes are faithfully echoed by Matthew in his gospel. When he tells the story of Jesus' miraculous birth, he is not at all concerned with Mary's reaction. All he appears interested in is what poor Joseph is going to think about Mary's sudden pregnancy. It is Paul's great disciple, Luke, who is certain that God would have announced his intentions to Mary first, as a matter of courtesy, and who gives to women in his gospel complete spiritual parity. But Luke is also adamant that any serious Christian will leave his wife for Christ's sake, going further than his master Paul in this respect, and not even the chauvinist Matthew insists with such energy as Paul that woman is an inferior creature, that man is created for God only and she for God in man.

There is real rancour in Paul's insistence that it would serve a woman right if she had her hair shaved off for failing to wear a veil. The stridency in the way he repeats himself suggests that the behaviour of the Corinthian women had touched in Paul some nerve of dislike that is against his better theological judgement. His attitude here goes against one of the fundamental principles of his gospel. He brings to a close the veil question with a refusal to discuss the matter any further: 'To anyone who might still want to argue: it is not the custom with us, nor in the churches of God' (1 Corinthians 11:16) – a rather lame argument which suggests that Paul knew he was on thin ice theologically.

Most of the time Paul was able to keep his misogyny under control; only in his first Epistle to the Corinthians does it surface. Later Christians, of course, have not been so restrained, and they have seen in Paul's writing a justification for their own prejudices. Tertullian said that women were the gateways to Hell and criminals at the divine bar. Augustine said that they were full of excrement. When St Bernard's sister went to visit him at Clairvaux wearing a new dress, Bernard flew into a rage and called her a filthy whore. One can merely wonder at the repressed souls of these Christian celibates, for whom women could be only temptation.

After leaving Corinth on his first, eighteen-month visit, Paul went to Ephesus briefly before returning to Judaea and to Antioch. Then he set out again, visiting Asia Minor and his churches there, and staying in Ephesus at the end of his third and last great missionary journey. Ephesus, where Paul intended to set up a centre of missionary activities in Asia Minor, quickly produced a number of converts. As usual and as happened in Corinth, Paul began his preaching in the synagogues; then after he was ejected he moved out into lecture rooms, in the house of Tyrannus. Luke makes out that Paul's stay in Ephesus was one of undiluted triumph. He was so successful that the silversmiths who made silver shrines of Diana were put out of business:

> 'Now you must have seen and heard how, not just in Ephesus but nearly everywhere in Asia, this man Paul has persuaded and converted a great number of people with his argument that gods made by hand are not gods at all. This threatens not only to discredit our trade but also to reduce the sanctuary of the great goddess Diana to unimportance. It could end up by taking away all the prestige of a goddess venerated all over Asia, yes, and everywhere in the civilised world.' This speech roused them to fury and they started to shout, 'Great is Diana of the Ephesians'.
>
> (Acts 19: 26-28)

Paul's stay in Ephesus was not successful, though we have to rely on a few scattered remarks in the letters about 'great opposition' (1 Corinthinans 16: 9) to give an indication of this. It was certainly not successful enough to endanger the great cult of Diana at Ephesus, but strangely enough Luke was writing more prophetically than he knew. The great temple of Diana at Ephesus has long been obliterated and archaeologists have still not discovered it. From what we can gather at Ephesus, Diana was worshipped not only in her normal virginal capacity; she was also goddess of fertility. In effigies and statues her breasts were replaced by numberless small eggs.

In the fifth century the Christian council of Ephesus met to discuss some of the problems raised by the heretic Nestorius about the doctrine of the Incarnation. Nestorius held that there was a division in Jesus' nature between the human and the divine. Mary was not the mother of the God-part of Jesus, but only the mother of the man Jesus. The council declared this to be heresy. There was no such split in the nature of Christ. When Mary conceived Jesus she conceived him not only as man but God also. The council declared solemnly that Mary was Theotokos, the Mother of

God. As we have seen, neither Paul nor the synoptic Gospels were familiar with this idea. For them Jesus had been conceived as a normal human being, and while he had lived on earth he had been an ordinary man.

The Christians at Ephesus were delighted with the council's decision. They carried Mary's effigy through the streets in a huge torchlight procession. In Mary Theotokos they had a Christian replacement for Diana of Ephesus. Like Diana she was virgin and yet more fecund than any other woman in the world in that she had conceived and given birth to God himself. By this time, alas, it was too late for the Church to revise its opinions on women and on the body. The fact that a woman had carried God in her womb had already been felt by women-hating celibates of the early Church as an embarrassment. They had insisted that Mary remained a virgin not only before the birth of Christ but afterwards as well. Her hymen remained intact; it was not a normal birth. Christ may have been born of a woman, but the Church wanted to make the birth as separate from a woman's dangerous womb as possible.

Although Paul was at first unsuccessful in Ephesus, later an important Pauline school of theology developed there. There the post-Pauline Epistles Colossians and Ephesians, and the pastoral letters to Timothy and Titus were written. Ephesians has been dated at AD 100, and here we can see an interesting but ominous development. By this time the Church had greatly expanded, and Paul's unified vision of a structured institution, united by one belief in his gospel, had become more of a reality. Paul, as we have seen, used the image of the Christian community as the 'body of Christ', and the Pauline writers of Ephesus continue this tradition. But there is now an important difference. In Corinthians, when the individual Christians ate the bread of the Eucharist, they became, each one of them, united in the body of Christ. Paul meant this quite literally; by baptism

Christians had literally participated in Christ's death and were literally members of his risen body. 'Saul, Saul, why do you persecute me?' Christ had asked him on the road to Damascus, seeing himself united to his followers on earth – he suffering in them and they in him.

The author of the Epistle to the Ephesians also uses this image. However, for him the body of Christ is the Church, and Christ is its head. There is a separation of Christ and the Church, with the Church moving into the middle of the picture, ousting the individual Christian. The author of Colossians make the same distinction:

> Now the Church is his body. He is its head.
>
> (Colossians 1: 18)

In a great and celebrated passage, which contains the most positive statement about women and about sex in the whole Pauline corpus, the author of Ephesians places the Church centre stage. Christ deals only with the Church, not with the individual Christians; in this image he loves the Church, cherishes the Church and instead of Christians being his body, he is now the head, superior to and separate from the Church:

> Give way to one another in obedience to Christ. Wives should regard their husbands as they regard the Lord, since Christ is the head of the Church and saves the whole body, so is a husband the head of his wife; and as the Church submits to Christ, so should wives to their husbands in everything. Husbands should love their wives just as Christ loved the Church and sacrificed himself for her to make her holy. He made her clean by washing her in water with a form of words, so that when he took her to himself she would be glorious, with no speck or wrinkle or anything like that but holy and faultless. In the same way husbands must love their wives as they love their own bodies; for a man to love his wife is for him to love himself. A man never hates his own body, but he feeds it and looks after it; and that is the way

Christ treats the Church, because it is his body – and we are its living parts.

(Ephesians 5: 21-31)

Although the author stresses the love and unity that exist between Christ and the Church, there is now a separation between them, not the simple unity that there was before. The Church submits to Christ as a woman submits to her husband. Woman is still felt to be the inferior creature that Paul considered her, even though she is the symbol of such a reality. She needs considerable purification before she will be fit for her husband. It is the Church who is saved, the Church who is fed and cherished by Christ, not the individual Christians. This is a dangerous of step of reasoning, though an inevitable one, given the problems of administering an international institution into the close unity envisaged by Paul. Once the institution has upstaged the individual, we have institutional problems and politics; the institution starts to interpose itself between the Christian and his God. Paul's authoritarian stance, his insistence on a solidly united Church believing in one gospel, is developed by his immediate successors into an exaltation of the institution itself. We know only too well what later Christians have done with this ideal.

Paul left Ephesus to return to Jerusalem. Just as the evangelists present Christ as going up to Jerusalem to court death deliberately, just as Christ prophesies his Passion, so too, according to Luke, did Paul. At Miletus, he made a highly emotional speech which reduced the Ephesian elders to tears, saying that he had no idea what lay ahead for him, 'except that the Holy Spirit, in town after town, has made it clear enough that imprisonment and persecution await me' (Acts 20: 23). He was now certain 'that none of you among whom I have gone about proclaiming the kingdom will ever see my face again' (Acts 20: 25). The disciples at Tyre, when they finally reached Judaea, begged Paul not to go to

Jerusalem, 'speaking in the Spirit' (Acts 21: 4).

At Caesarea, a prophet called Agabas took Paul's girdle and bound his own feet and hands, saying, 'The man this girdle belongs to will be bound like this by the Jews in Jerusalem, and handed over to the Pagans' (Acts 21: 11). It is exactly what the evangelists claim happened to Christ. Paul, of course, took no notice of these warnings:

> When we heard this, we and everybody there implored Paul not to go to Jerusalem. To this he replied, 'What are you trying to do, weaken my resolution by your tears? For my part I am ready not only to be tied up but even to die in Jerusalem for the name of the Lord Jesus.
>
> (Acts 21: 13-14)

Paul's awareness of the dangers he would face in Judaea may be seen in his writing to the Romans begging them to pray 'that I may escape the unbelievers in Judaea, and that the aid that I carry to Jerusalem may be accepted by the saints' (Romans 15: 31). He was taking with him the collection for the poor which James had asked him to make eight years before, during the circumcision discussions. He was now ready to present it to the Jerusalem church, to make a bid for reconciliation. This was an important, indeed crucial, mission for him, and he was ready to brave whatever befell him in Judaea.Such an interpretation is far more likely than that Paul was deliberately walking into his own death for no apparent reason, which is what Luke's narrative suggests. Luke did not want to reveal that there was any need for reconciliation at all, because according to him there had never been a conflict.

By the time Luke was writing, at the end of the first century, such a deliberate seeking out of martyrdom was becoming a vogue in the Church.

6 The Christian way of death

When Paul returned to Jerusalem after his last missionary journey, he was in effect beginning another journey, which would lead ultimately to his death. For the last eight years he had been coaxing from his converts a collection of money for the 'saints' in Jerusalem. This was a way of acknowledging the link between Paul's gentile churches and their Judaic roots. Now he was bringing the collection, rather apprehensively, to Jerusalem.

Luke conceals the tenseness of the occasion. Paul and his party received a 'very warm welcome' from the brothers in Jerusalem (Acts 21: 17) as Paul gave James an account of his pagan conversions, which was well received. However, James and the elders, Luke has to admit, did have a worry:

'But you see, brother,' they said, 'how thousands of Jews have now become believers, all of them staunch upholders of the Law, and they have heard that you instruct all Jews living among the pagans to break away from Moses, authorising them not to circumcise their children or to follow the customary practices. What is to be done? Inevitably, there will be a meeting of the whole body, since they are bound to hear that you have come. So do as we suggest. We have four men here who are under a vow; take these men along and be purified with them and pay all the expenses connected with the shaving of their heads. This will let everyone know there is no truth in the reports they have heard about you and that you still regularly observe the Law.'

(Acts 21: 20-24)

We have no idea how James really received Paul nor whether the meeting was as amicable as Luke makes out. Acts of the Apostles is now our only source, for no further Epistles of Paul have survived from after he arrived in Jerusalem.

The feast when Paul participated in the purification ceremonies in the Temple was the feast of Pentecost, which celebrates the giving of the Torah to Israel. The Law, which the Jews held to be necessary for salvation, Paul had now declared obsolete, and unnecessary for gentile converts who had been baptised into the death of Christ. Paul would have felt no difficulty about attending these rites of purification and taking part in the ceremony himself. He would not have considered it a compromise. Earlier he had written:

> So though I am not a slave of any man I have made myself the slave of everyone so as to win as many as I could. I made myself a Jew to the Jews, to win the Jews; that is, I who am not a subject of the Law made myself a subject of the Law to those who are the subjects of the Law, to win those who are subject to the Law. To those who have no Law, I was free of the Law myself (though not free from God's Law, being under the Law of Christ) to win those who have no Law. For the weak, I made myself weak. I made myself all things to all men in order to save some at any cost; and I still do this, for the sake of the gospel, to have a share in its blessings.
>
> (1 Corinthians 9: 19-23)

This policy of being 'all things to all men' is not just a spirit of compromise for the sake of making converts. It is not a sacrifice of integrity. It is a policy central to Paul's conception of Christianity. Paul, the Christian, who had been made a 'new creation' in Christ, (2 Corinthians 5: 17) no longer had the standpoints that the natural man needs to define himself. Christ had freed him from these limits, because in Christ there is neither Jew nor gentile. This Pauline concept of freedom is not a sloppy liberalism, but a hard discipline of abandoning natural prejudices and inclinations. It is a death to self for the sake of the gospel and his mission, the paramount concerns of Paul's life.

When Paul went to the Temple to make himself subject to the Law for the sake of the Jews, he was arrested. His presence in the Temple provoked a riot, similar to the one fourteen years before when Stephen was stoned to death. The Jews, when they saw Paul, had almost exactly the same objections as they had to Stephen: 'Men of Israel, help! This is the man who preaches to everyone everywhere against our people, against the Law and against this place' (Acts 21: 28). There is a symmetry in Luke's account. Paul's first appearance on the Christian scene had been to preside over Stephen's stoning. His last appearance as a free man was to be arrested himself and threatened with instant death in the Temple for the same reasons as Stephen. He was not killed, because the Romans in the Fortress Antonia, which overlooked the Temple area, rushed out and saved him by a show of military force.

Luke suggests that the Jews thought that Paul had brought into the sacred precincts of the Temple, where gentiles were forbidden entrance, one of his uncircumcised converts, Trophemus from Ephesus. Paul had brought the uncircumcised Titus with him to force the issue of circumcision on the Jerusalem church eight years earlier; but to act so provocatively now, when he was on a mission of reconciliation, would have been truly foolhardy. It is more likely that Paul's views on the annulment of the old covenant with Israel were considered such blasphemy that his mere presence in the Temple sparked off an explosion of feeling.

What did the Jewish Christians in Judaea do with their fellow Jews to try to help Paul? Not very much, according to Luke. For them, Paul's views would have been at best an embarrassment, trying as they were to function as a sect within Judaism. Writing of the perils of his missionary life,

Paul included the perils he endured from 'so-called brothers' as though his co-religionists were hounding him as well as the Jews. Clement of Rome, writing in AD 96, says that Paul died because of 'jealousy and contention'. This has led scholars to suggest that this was an internal conflict within Christianity, rather than a confrontation with the Jews, who, though they would have disapproved of Paul, would have had no reason to be 'jealous'. Could it be that the Jewish Christians connived at Paul's death, seeing, as good Jews, that his views were more than a danger to their sect, a terrible blasphemy? We have no evidence to support this view, and it remains a matter for speculation.

Apparently not all the Jews were opposed to Paul. During his meeting with the Sanhedrin after his arrest, Paul enlisted the support of the Pharisees by claiming that as a 'Pharisee and the son of Pharisees' he was on trial for their common hope in the resurrection of the dead. This created instant division in the ranks and absolute chaos:

> As soon as he said this a dispute broke out between the Pharisees and the Sadducees and the assembly was split between two parties. For the Sadducees say there is neither resurrection, nor angel, nor spirit, while the Pharisees accept all three. The shouting grew louder, and some of the scribes from the Pharisees party stood up and protested strongly, 'We find nothing wrong with this man. Suppose a spirit has spoken to him, or an angel?' Feeling was running high, and the tribune, fearing that they would tear Paul to pieces, ordered his troops to go down and haul him out and bring him to the fortress.

(Acts 23: 7-10)

Paul's clever move to split the opposition – he would have been aware of the Pharisees' 'wait and see' attitude – worked well. It made the Romans, already horrified to discover that they had put a Roman citizen in chains, even more uncertain what to do with Paul. If even the Jews were undecided about him, how could they, who found nothing with which to charge him, convict them? They were anxious to go along with the Jews where possible to prevent trouble, but which Jews should they go along with?

Paul's tactics here show that, unlike the Jesus of the gospels, he was not passive at his trial. Luke has suggested that Paul went up to Jerusalem deliberately to court death, just as Jesus did, but his long account of Paul before the Jewish as well as the Roman authorities shows Paul battling for his life. There is a strong resemblance, as we have seen, between the way Luke presents Paul's arrest and trial and the way the evangelists show Jesus being arrested and tried. Their predicament was the same; both were arrested by the Jews and handed over to the Romans. But there the similarity ends. In the gospels, Jesus refused to speak when he appeared before the Sanhedrin and before Pilate. On the few occasions when he did speak he was deliberately provocative, seeming either to have given up or to actually want to be crucified – which, according to the evangelists, he did. That was how he was going to save the world. Later Christians would imitate Christ's willingness to die in various ways, physical and spiritual, seeing Christ's passivity as holy. Yet Paul did not seem to have had this view at all. There was an occasion where Paul's trial and Jesus' became uncannily similar. Jesus had been deliberately insulting to the high priest and he was struck across the face: 'Is that the way to answer the high priest?' Jesus replied spiritedly, possibly making the situation worse: 'If there is something wrong in what I have said, point it out; but if there is no offence in it, why do you strike me?' (John 18: 23.) Paul's reaction was quite different:

> Paul looked steadily at the Sanhedrin and began to speak, 'My brothers, to this day I have conducted myself before God with a perfectly clear conscience.' At this the high priest, Ananias, ordered his attendants to strike him on the

mouth. Then Paul said to him, 'God will surely strike you, you whitewashed wall! How can you sit there and judge me according to the Law, and then break the Law by ordering a man to strike me?' The attendants said, 'It is God's high priest you are insulting!' Paul answered, 'Brothers, I did not realise it was the high priest, for scripture says: *You must not curse a ruler of your people.*[1]

(Acts 23: 1-5)

The point here is that Paul did not think an apology out of place. He did consider his Christian duty was to die as soon as possible a martyr for the faith. He was fighting for his life, not out of cowardice – no one could accuse Paul of that – but because he believed in using every means he could to get himself out of danger.

There followed a deadlock. The Romans found him an embarrassment. They could not find anything wrong with this exceptional Jew, who was a Roman citizen and also a strong supporter of the empire. Paul was imprisoned at Caesarea, according to Luke, for two years, while the Romans, not wanting to offend the Jews, feared to release Paul because he was likely to be lynched the moment he left the safety of prison. Paul apparently broke the deadlock. He had had one of his visions: 'The Lord appeared to him and said, "Courage! You have borne witness for me in Jerusalem, now you must do the same in Rome" ' (Acts 23: 11).

Paul asked to be tried in Rome by Caesar, as was his right as a Roman citizen. It appeared to most people that if Paul hung on he would probably be acquitted, so this seemed a stupid move which could be interpreted as visionary hysteria. It is tempting to speculate on his reasons for asking to go to Rome to have his case tried by, of all people, Nero. Was this one of the times when vision was succeeded by sensible idea? For years he had been trying to get to Rome. Here was an opportunity. There would be no more harassment from

1. Exodus 22: 27.

Jews; the travelling conditions would be excellent – Luke says Paul was a privileged prisoner who was allowed to stay with friends *en route*, and could even take a party with him. As there was nothing in his gospel that was opposed to Rome, he would probably be acquitted, and he could then visit the Roman church as had long been his intention. From Rome it was really no distance to Spain; he could establish the gospel at the ends of the earth and then it would be time for the *parousia*. Christ was waiting only for him to finish his mission.

Festus, who was Roman governor by that time, supported Paul's plan, probably seeing this as a good way out of the difficulty, and insisted that Paul be transferred to Rome. Paul finally left the Holy Land for the last time. On each of his missionary journeys he had returned there; for him it was precious because it was the land of his fathers, the land which had produced Christ, whom Israel had been so long expecting. He must have felt a sadness that it was his own people who were casting him out. He must have known that Judaism would never be able to accept his gospel fully, but as far as we know he never abandoned hope that they would finally be converted. He never rejected Judaism; inevitably, Judaism rejected him.

After an eventful voyage, which included the famous shipwreck at Malta, Paul arrived in Italy at Pozzuoli, on the bay of Naples, and stayed there for a week. Although he was an ardent champion of the empire, the decadence of much Roman life disgusted him:

> . . . since they refused to see it was rational to acknowledge God, God has left them to their own irrational ideas and to their monstrous behaviour. And so they are steeped in all sorts of depravity, rottenness, greed, malice and addicted to envy, murder, wrangling, treachery and spite. Libellers, slanderers, enemies of God, rude, arrogant and boastful, enterprising in sin, rebellious to parents, without brains,

honour, love or pity. They know what God's verdict is: that those who behave like this deserve to die – and yet they do it; and what is worse, encourage others to do the same.

(Romans 1: 28-32)

Once in Italy Paul encountered Roman life at first hand. Many pagans, we know, were having recourse to the mystery religions at this time, as disgusted and as disillusioned as Paul with the pointlessness of their lives. Yet when we look at some of the Roman villas in the area we see another side of Roman life, a life firmly embedded in this world. Most of us who either are Christians or who have been, however remotely, touched by the Christian message probably find the luxury of Roman villa life acceptable. Their antiquity removes them safely to the world of art and culture. But when we are presented with sensuous pleasure more immediately, many of us feel at least a flicker of unease. Response to pleasure reminds us that we are far too enslaved to a world we are supposed to have left behind. And yet if we cannot live fully in the world, where can we live? Ultimately, if we reject the world we have, in some sense, to die.

In the Roman villas of the time, in Pompeii for example, which is very near Pozzuoli, where Paul spent his first week in Italy, we see life organised around the principle of beauty. The resources of the natural world and the skill of man have been exploited to manufacture pleasure. Like it or not, we are sensuous creatures and our senses respond spontaneously to pleasure. Often the Christian attitude to pleasure seems churlish; and ingratitude to the God who presumably gave man his ability to respond to and to exploit beauty and pleasure. If we close the gateways of our senses, as we have seen, we can no longer be fed by our environment and will ultimately wither away, impoverished beings.

Paul was an ascetic. His life of missionary hardship, which he describes so graphically, would probably have made him despise the luxurious lives of the Romans. He constantly describes himself as a Christian athlete, in vigorous training for Heaven and the future glorification of the *parousia*:

> All the runners in the stadium are trying to win, but only one gets the prize. You must run in the same way, meaning to win. All the fighters at the games go into strict training; they do this just to win a wreath that will wither away, but we do it for a wreath that will never wither. That is how I run, intent on winning; that is how I fight, not beating the air. I treat my body hard and make it obey me, for, having been an announcer myself, I should not want to be disqualified.

(1 Corinthians 9: 24-27)

The Christian life, according to Paul, is a life of strain. The Christian is fighting, running, training himself away from a world which is withering away. The softness of a life of sensuous pleasure is not for him.

Yet Jesus does not seem to have shared this attitude. It is true that he lived a tough mendicant life: 'foxes have holes, birds have their nests, but the Son of Man has nowhere to lay his head' (Luke 9: 58). Yet he does not appear to have despised pleasure when it was offered. He called his disciples to a life of hardship, but the gospels frequently show him going to dinner with the leading Pharisees; and though he is sometimes presented as behaving rudely to his hosts on these occasions, he is not horrified by the luxury or pleasure of his meal. He is reported to have urged his disciples to sit freely to wealth, to give it away, and not to be concerned with hoarding possessions. However, he was not an ascetic like Paul, nor like John the Baptist. One gospel saying attributed to Jesus shows that this fact was noted by his contemporaries:

> What description, then, can I find for the men of this generation? What are they like? They are like children shouting to one another while they sit in the market place:

'We played the pipes for you,
and you wouldn't dance;
we sang dirges
and you wouldn't cry.'

For John the Baptist comes, not eating bread, not drinking wine, and you say 'he is possessed'. The Son of Man comes, eating and drinking, and you say, 'Look, a glutton and a drunkard, a friend of tax collectors and sinners.

(Luke 7: 31-34)

Paul's asceticism has stamped Christianity, more than Jesus' occasional enjoyment of the world.

In the mystery religions, many pagans also sought to leave the world and discover a new realm of experience. The initiates were sworn to secrecy, so we have little idea of what went on in the ceremonies, but one of the most tantalising glimpses that we have comes from Apulius, who quotes for us the experience of one Lucius. Through these little-known rites, Lucius was taken right out of this world:

'You, O zealous reader, will perhaps ask eagerly enough what was then said and done. I would tell you if I might, but ear and tongue would incur the same guilt of rash inquisitiveness. Yet I will not torture you with long suspense, when you are perhaps aglow with pious yearning. So hear, yes, and believe the things that are true. I visited the bounds of death. I trod Proserpina's threshold. I passed through all the elements and returned. It was midnight, but I saw the sun radiant with bright light. I came into the very presence of the gods below and the gods above and I adored them face to face.'

(*Metamorphoses* xi, 23)

Like many other initiates, Lucius has ceremonially died into life. He has achieved union with the gods. Often the ceremonial seems to have been of a dubiously sensual nature designed to convey impressively the union with the divine achieved by the initiate. Lucius worshipped the gods 'face to face', a state which Paul explicitly says, in his well-known hymn on charity (1 Corinthians 13:12), will be reserved for the *parousia*, or after death.

If Lucius escaped the world and entered a cosmic reality, the Christian according to Paul has not yet fully escaped it; by means of an asceticism he is straining away from the world, but he will achieve glorification only in the next life. The mysteries were also individualistic, whereas Paul insists on the common bond and tasks that Christians have, once they have been incorporated into the body of Christ. Sometimes the Epistles use the word 'mystery', but for Paul the mystery would not be fully revealed in this life. This, in another form, had been Paul's quarrel with the Enthusiasts at Corinth. For Paul, Christianity is a way of death, Christ's death:

> You have been taught that when we were baptised in Christ Jesus we were baptised in his death; in other words, when we were baptised we went into the tomb with him and joined him in death, so that as Christ was raised from the dead by the Father's glory, we too might live a new life.
>
> If in union with Christ we have imitated his death, we shall also imitate him in his resurrection. We must realise that our former selves have been crucified with him to destroy this sinful body and to free us from the slavery of sin. When a man dies, of course, he has finished with sin.
>
> But we believe that having died with Christ we shall return to life with him: Christ as we know having been raised from the dead will never die again. Death has no more power over him any more. When he died, he died, once for all, to sin, so his life now is life with God; and in that way, you too must consider yourselves to be dead to sin but alive for God in Christ Jesus.

(Romans 6:1-11)

It is probable that the first Christians who adopted the Jewish ritual of baptism spoke of dying with Jesus symbolically, but it was Paul, as far as we know, who developed this concept fully. The Christian has died in baptism; it is an accomplished fact. He will rise again with Christ, but the verbs in the above passage that speak of resurrection look to the future. Full glorification, resurrection and union with God are not for this life. In this brief interim before the *parousia* Christians are living out Christ's death.

Similarly in the Eucharist, Paul gives Christ's death central importance. It would seem that for the Jewish Christians it was an eschatological rite; a drinking to the new convenant in Jesus, and a looking forward to his return. He himself is reported to have said at the last supper: 'Amen, amen, I shall not drink the fruit of the vine again, until I drink it with you as new wine in the Kingdom of my Father' (Matthew 26: 29). He was looking forward to the messianic banquet which was a popular image and theme. For Paul the Eucharist is all these things too, but it is also a reminder of the Lord's death: 'Until the Lord comes, therefore, every time you eat this bread and drink this cup, you are proclaiming his death' (1 Corinthians 11: 26-27). Again, when he was defending his apostleship to the Corinthians, Paul made suffering the sign of the true apostle: 'Always, wherever we may be we carry with us in our body the death of Jesus' (2 Corinthians 4: 10). Only thus will the Christian one day receive the life of Jesus. Paul, then, cannot be said to have created a new mystery religion. His stress on the death of the Christian separates his gospel irrevocably from the pagan mysteries practised at the time.

Paul had already written to the Christians in Rome his great theological manifesto, and from his letter we can gather that in the Roman church there were a number of Jewish Christians, who inclined towards the Torah, as well as a number of gentile converts. These two groups tended to look down on one another. The number of Jewish Christians in the Roman church supports historically the old

Christian tradition that St Peter founded the church in Rome. But, although this has been very convenient for the papacy, it is difficult to accord the tradition much validity.

There is a pious Christian legend that as Paul approached Rome a number of Christians, headed by his old enemy St Peter, came out to greet him, and that on the Via Appia the two apostles embraced lovingly. There is no warrant for this, however. If it had happened Luke would certainly have mentioned it with a great fanfare as a perfect example of the unity of the early Church. As it is, his narrative stops when he gets Paul to Rome. He never once mentions Peter's presence in Rome, which he would certainly have done had he known of it. Paul, he says, lived for two years in the city in a rented lodging, 'proclaiming the truth about the Lord Jesus with complete freedom and without hindrance from anybody' (Acts 28: 31). We know Luke to be pro-Roman, and he is unlikely to have wanted to mention that Paul was probably executed during the persecution of Nero, anxious as always to portray the Romans as early admirers of Christianity.

'Probably' is an important proviso. We have no knowledge at all of how Paul met his death, or whether he really did die at Rome. Tradition preserves the prison, where Peter and Paul were supposedly incarcerated together, and legend has it that they converted the gaoler, something that we have seen happening in Acts of the Apostles. Yet this is all legend. It seems more likely that Paul did die in Rome under Nero, who blamed the Christians for the city's great fires; and if Paul was still in Rome during the mid 60s, he would, as a Christian ringleader, almost certainly have been executed. This tradition seems more likely than the more rosy one that Paul got to Spain after all and completed his mission.

Legends may not tell us the historical truth, but as we have seen in Acts they can tell us other truths about Christianity. The legend of Peter's death, which was written down in the twelfth century, expresses an important Christian attitude, whether or not the story is historically true. Peter too is believed to have died in Rome under Nero. The legend says that Peter was smuggled out of Rome by his fellow Christians, and that he managed to escape the city. Once outside the walls of the city, however, he met Jesus, walking in the opposite direction, carrying a cross. 'Lord,' Peter asked him, 'where are you going?' (Domine, quo vadis?) 'I am going to Rome,' Christ replied, 'to be crucified for a second time.' Peter understood. During Christ's earthly life he had frequently been chided for his worldly attitude. When Jesus had announced that he was going up to Jerusalem to be put to death and had prophesied his Passion in detail, Peter was horrified and protested vehemently against such a fate for his master. Jesus had rounded on him viciously: 'Get thou behind me, Satan.' Again on the night that Jesus was arrested, Peter had denied Jesus three times, to save his own skin. Still, thirty years later, he hadn't learnt his lesson. His duty was not to attempt to save his own life, but to return and as a Christian leader die with his flock. Tearful and contrite, Peter returned to Rome to a voluntary death.

Considerations like the fact that Peter might be more use to the Church alive than dead are mere worldly rationalisations. That kind of thinking all too often masks cowardice and our innate and unworthy sense of self-preservation, an egotistical shield against hurt and destruction. That should not be the Christian attitude. The Christian attacks this self-love head on, going forward voluntarily to embrace his own death, whether he is privileged to die as a martyr or not.

When the time came for Peter to die, he asked to be crucified upside down. His master, he said, had come from Heaven and so could be crucified with his head pointing to Heaven, but he, Peter, had come from the earth and should be crucified with his head pointing towards the ground. The new Christian heroism is not a heroism of self-aggrandisement, but a heroism of humility and death to self. It is a heroism not of action, but of suffering. Unlike the worldly man, the Christian has to imitate Christ who voluntarily went forward to meet death. Like Peter, the Christian should not try to avoid suffering, but should go out to suffer as much as possible. That way his victory over the world is complete, his victory of spirit over the shrinking and sensual body which is always clinging to the earth. It is better to put it to death entirely and follow Jesus right up to the last agony. Such was the Christian attitude to martyrdom, expressed poignantly in the *quo vadis* story, but how far is this attitude a distortion of the way Jesus saw his own death and as such a distortion of Christianity?

Judaism had had its martyrs too. The Book of Maccabees tells of the proud death of those who died for the Law and for Israel under Antiochus Epiphanes. In Judaism, however, it seems that martyrdom was purely defensive, something to be accepted bravely if necessary, but not a fate to be deliberately sought. The muddled gospel accounts of Jesus' death show him going forward to his death; he foretold it in detail and brought it upon himself. It is thus that he saved the world. Yet there is a well-attested gospel story that just after the Last Supper, when his arrest and death appeared inevitable, Jesus prayed in an agony in Gethsemane on the Mount of Olives, sweat pouring off him like drops of blood: 'My father, if it be possible, let this cup pass me by, nevertheless, not as I will but as thou wilt' (Mark 14: 36). This would suggest that he accepted the Judaic view of martyrdom, rather than the later Christian one.

Once Christianity ceased to be part of Judaism, it no longer enjoyed the Jews' religious freedom in the empire, becoming a target for persecution when Christians refused to sacrifice to the emperor. Martyrdom quickly became the way of following Christ most perfectly. A martyr was in fact the Church's most useful asset: 'The blood of martyrs is the seed of Christians,' wrote Tertullian, and, indeed, it became a sign of virtue to denounce yourself to the authorities and be flung to the lions.

The most eloquent of these early martyrs was St Ignatius, Bishop of Antioch. He was martyred in the year 107, and was brought from Antioch to Rome for this purpose. Antioch, we have seen, was a church with Pauline connections, and Ignatius was a great admirer of Paul. *En route* to martyrdom he wrote various letters to the different churches like Paul, urging them to remain in the faith. One of these letters was to the Roman church, which was trying to get Ignatius acquitted. Ignatius implored them not to do so:

> For my part, I am writing to all the churches and assuring them that I am truly in earnest about dying for God – if only you yourselves put no obstacles in the way. I must implore you to do me no such untimely kindness; pray leave me to be a meal for the beasts, for it is they who can provide my way to God. I am His wheat, ground fine by the lion's teeth to be made purest bread for Christ. Better still, incite the creatures to become a sepulchre for me; let them not leave the smallest scrap of my flesh, so that I need not be a burden to anyone after I fall asleep. When there is no trace of my body left for the world to see, then I shall truly be Jesus Christ's disciple.

(*Ignatian Epistles*, Romans 4)

Only when his body has completely disappeared in a hideous death will he really be following Jesus. There is no passivity here; Christians are meant to pull their deaths upon themselves, 'inciting' the lions to do their worst. Ignatius writes that he is going to coax the lions to be as savage as possible; if they show any reluctance he will 'use force in them'. With enormous enthusiasm Ignatius lists the horrors that might lie in store for him: 'Fire, the cross, beast-fighting, hacking and quartering, splintering of bone and mangling of limb, even pulverising of my entire body –

let every horrid and diabolical torment come upon me, provided only that that I can win my way to Jesus Christ!' (*Ignatiau Epistles*, Romans 5.) Only if he suffers in the worst way possible has he a hope of winning Jesus Christ and a glorious afterlife:

> Here and now as I write in the fullness of life, I am yearning for death with all the passion of a lover. Earthly longings have been crucified; in me there is left no spark of desire for mundane things, but only a murmur of living water that whispers within me, 'Come to the Father.'

(*Ignatian Epistles*, Romans 7)

Anyone who has once been caught by this ideal will respond to the seductive beauty in these words. Yet something unhealthy is present when the fullness of life, the passion of love and springs of living water speak only of death.

When Christianity became the state religion of Rome, martyrdom could no longer be the perfect way to follow Christ. The Church had outlawed voluntary martyrdom, but not the underlying ideal. Nowhere is this more clearly seen than in the haste with which Christians sought a substitute for martyrdom. There had to be a way for the ambitious Christian to imitate Christ in his death on the Cross. In the gospels he had said that a serious Christian had to take up his cross and follow him to death, and with martyrdom at an end, Christians chose monasticism as the new means to that end. The early monks and the fathers of the desert inflicted horrible tortures on their bodies. St Antony beat his body black and blue till the blood ran, starved himself till he looked like a scarecrow and drove himself by his asceticism into a state of hysteria, where he saw visions of devils and wicked women. In England, Celtic monks immersed themselves in ice-cold water all night, chanting lengthy litanies. What the lions and the executioners had done swiftly, these monks performed on them-

selves, making their lives a daily martyrdom. Later, under St
Benedict, the physical penance was mitigated and monks
were told to die to themselves spiritually, but the ideal of
death persisted. Until quite recently monks and nuns still
took the discipline, practised flagellation and wore hair
shirts. When a religious made his vows it was, until recently,
common for him to lie under a funeral pall in token of the
fact that he was now dead to the world and embracing a life
of daily dying.

It is not necessary to be a monk or a martyr to have
imbibed something of that ideal. Christianity, in many of its
forms, seems devoted to the principle of 'the nastier the
better'. Hair shirts and disciplines are just symbols of an
attitude to life that turns away from the world, crucifies
earthly delights, turns guiltily away from pleasure, and
manufactures suffering. Yet this is a contradiction in terms.
The word 'suffering' implies passivity; things are done to
you, you do not bring it about yourself. Surely life is quite
painful enough and offers plenty of opportunities for suffering without our deliberately going out of our way to
create new horrors for ourselves.

The person indirectly responsible for this perversity of
Christian masochism is St Paul. It was he who put suffering
into the heart of the Christian life. It was he who wrote
movingly of the folly of the Cross, he who urged Christianity to renounce the world, he who preached only about
Christ crucified. It seems that pre-Pauline Christianity saw
the Cross as a passing episode for Jesus – Christ had died a
martyr for Israel, but he had risen again and would return in
glory. The imminent coming of the kingdom gave Christianity an eschatological thrust. Paul's disputes with the
Judaisers and the Enthusiasts led him in his letters to stress
the power and beauty of the Cross and to preach a Christian
life that was a way of death.

To be fair to Paul, he did not have Ignatius' attitude of

deliberately bringing down suffering on his own head. He made enthusiastic lists of his past sufferings, just as Ignatius gleefully makes a list of his future torments. But there is an essential difference between the two: for Paul, the sufferings were sufferings, incidental to his mission, and it was the mission that came first not the courting of pain. We have seen that unlike Ignatius he fought for his life, before the Romans and the Sanhedrin. Although he can write 'for me to live is Christ, to die is gain' (Philippians 1: 21), he immediately qualifies this by saying that as there is so much work still to be done on the mission, to stay alive is a more urgent need:

> . . . if living in the body means doing work which is having good results – I do not know what I should choose. I am caught in this dilemma: I want to be gone and be with Christ, which would be very much the better, but for me to stay alive in this body is a more urgent need for your sake. This weighs with me so much that I feel sure I shall survive and stay with you all and help you to progress in the faith and even increase your joy in it; and so you will have another reason to give praise to Christ Jesus on my account when I am with you again.

> (Philippians 1: 22-26)

If Paul buffeted his body to make it his slave (1 Corinthians 9: 27) he was not beating himself with a discipline, flagellating himself in a monastic cell, though his words have led Christians to do so. He was living rough because the mission demanded it.

As a Roman citizen Paul had the privilege of being beheaded rather than having to endure the slow agonies of crucifixion. The church at the monastery at Tre Fontana is the traditional site of Paul's execution; with real Christian gruesomeness it displays the blood in a dark red patch on the floor, and shows the three fountains that sprang up where his head bounced three times after it was struck from his body. Instead of seeing his death as a glorious triumph, it is possible that Paul felt a failure. He had not completed his mission; the Cross of Christ had not been preached to the ends of the earth. He had suffered 'jealousy and contention' from his fellow Christians and had been rejected by Judaism. Some of his own converts had renounced his gospel. Now the empire which he had supported all his life was in the hands of a madman and was putting him to death. One can only hope that he did not lose his desire to leave the body and be with Christ. Years before he had looked forward to this moment:

> For we know in part and we prophesy in part; but when that which is perfect is come that which is in part, shall be done away . . . For now we see through a glass darkly, but then face to face. Now I know in part, but then I shall know even as I am known.
>
> (1 Corinthians 13: 10, 12)

What Paul could not have foreseen was the ultimate triumph of his gospel. He may be called the first Christian not only because he made Christianity break away from Judaism and become a gentile religion, but because he stamped Christianity with its theology – a theology that Jesus himself would perhaps have found surprising. Paul may have taken Christianity away from Judaism, but he never wanted to sever its links with the Jews. Thanks to him Christians today, who are not Jews, feel they have a link with the Old Testament. Paul took Christianity to the pagan world and his converts unconsciously adapted his gospel according to their own preconceptions. There is in many forms of Christianity a strong sense of pagan magic and superstition, as well as pagan forms of ritual. In addition, the fact that Christianity is in many societies part of the establishment, and that Christianity has been and still is a powerful political force, is, for good or ill, ultimately due to Paul. He wanted to make the Roman Empire accept Christianity, and established his churches in its administrative centres.

What Paul did for Christianity was provide it with a coherent theology, a system of thought. Christians may pray to Jesus, but they think about him in terms of Paul. On the rational foundation that he created out of an essentially irrational vision, other Christian thinkers – the evangelists, Augustine, Luther, Calvin and the rest – have built their own structures. Some of these Pauline theologies have been beneficial to Christianity, some have had a seductive beauty of their own and some have been unhealthy. Whatever one's judgement on this brilliant, energetic and perhaps disturbed man, it is now impossible to separate Paul from Christianity.

Epilogue

My worry about the implication of Paul's being the first Christian remains. Paul's faith does not rely on facts and reason. He is quite clear about this. Ordinary rational thinking cannot explain the mystery of the Cross. Paul was a visionary and his faith rested on a vision of Jesus which he then bequeathed to Christianity. For the visionary, facts and reason are unimportant. For those of us not visionaries they cannot be so easily ignored. When Paul asks us to share his vision of the risen Jesus who appeared to him on the road to Damascus, he tells us that what he calls the 'madness' of our faith will transform Jesus into the Lord, the Kyrios: his resurrection changed the historical Jesus into an exalted spiritual being with a new mission and a new significance.

Paul would not have been upset by my view of the historical Jesus, because he probably knew more about Jesus than any scholar today. He knew more about him and the circumstances of his life and death than the evangelists did, who all wrote their Gospels far later than Paul wrote his Epistles. He would not have considered for a moment that any of the researches of recent scholars invalidated his faith. Jesus as he had lived when he was 'in the flesh' was already for Paul an irrelevance. Paul was not an apostle because he had been rationally convinced by the facts of Jesus' death and resurrection, or because he had imbibed Jesus' teaching and thought the whole thing through logically and been converted. He was an Apostle because he had 'seen Jesus, our Lord' (1 Corinthians 9: 1). He had had a vision of Jesus as the Kyrios; Jesus had sent him to preach of this extra-ordinary good news to the pagans.

If we want to accept Christianity we have to share Paul's vision. Our faith cannot be based on reason, despite the current whittling down of those elements in Christianity hardest to believe and the long tradition of Christian apologetics which tries to prove Christian dogma rationally. Many people will choose to share Paul's vision and adopt it as their own. They will discover that the modern findings about the historical Jesus and the way he conceived his mission in no way affect their decision to believe Paul. Some will find it hard, even impossible, to accept another man's vision, however brilliantly and memorably expressed and however much admiration they have for Paul himself.

Table of significant events

Some of these dates will be a matter of controversy. Dating is made difficult by the lack of contemporary records and reliable dating for some of the events listed here.

BC

63	Pompey takes Jerusalem. The Idumaean Antipater rules Judaea.
50	*Wisdom* literature written in Alexandria.
48	Pompey killed after being defeated by Julius Caesar.
44	Murder of Julius Caesar.
38-37	Sosius, Roman governor of Syria, captures Jerusalem with the cooperation of Herod.
37-4	Herod the Great effectively king.
20-19	The winter sees the start of the rebuilding of the Temple.
	The Pharisees Hillel and Shammai teaching and founding their rival schools.
7	More than 6,000 Pharisees refuse to take the oath to Augustus on the occasion of a census.
7-6	Birth of Jesus.
4	Death of Herod.
	Rebellion in Jerusalem put down by Herod's son Archelaus, who then goes to Rome to appeal for the title of king.

Sabinus, procurator of Syria, comes to Jerusalem to make an inventory of the resources of Herod. Sharp opposition throughout the country.

Possible year of the rebellion of the Pharisee Saddok, who urged disobedience to Rome and refusal to pay taxes.

Sabinus appeals to the Roman legate in Syria, Varus, who pursues the rebels. 2,000 Pharisees crucified.

4   At the end of the year Augustus confirms Herod's last will.

Archelaus is ethnarch of Judaea and Samaria.

Herod Antipas tetrarch of Galilee and Peraea.

Philip tetrarch of the north-east

AD

6   Augustus deposes Archelaus, who is exiled to Gaul.

6-41   Judaea is a procuratorial province, with Caesarea as the capital and headquarters of the Roman governor.

5-10
(approx)   Birth of Paul at Tarsus in Cilicia.

14   Death of Augustus.

14-37   Tiberias is emperor.

18-36   The Roman governor of Judaea, Valerius Gratus, deposes the high priest Annas. Three other high priests follow. Then Caiphas becomes high priest in the year 18 and rules until 36.

26-36   Pontius Pilate governor of Judaea.

27   The preaching of John the Baptist.

29   John the Baptist imprisoned and executed by Herod Antipas. At about this time the ministry of Jesus.

30   On the eve of the Passover, Jesus is crucified.

On the feast of Pentecost the Holy Spirit descends on his apostles, who start to preach. The foundation of the Jewish Christian church in Jerusalem.

35	Pilate orders the massacre of the Samaritans on their holy mountain, Gerazim. He is recalled to Rome to justify his conduct and dies a violent death (execution or suicide).
36	Martyrdom of Stephen and the subsequent persecution.
	The Hellenistic Jewish Christians flee to the diaspora and take the good news of the gospel with them. The church at Antioch is founded.
	Conversion of Paul on the road to Damascus.
37	Death of Tiberias.
37-41	Caligula is emperor.
36-39	Paul in the Arabian desert.
	Then Paul goes to Damascus.
39	After his escape from King Aretas, Paul visits the Jewish Christian church and meets only Peter and James.
41	Assassination of Caligula.
41-54	Claudius is emperor.
43	Barnabas brings Paul to Antioch.
45-49?	Paul's first missionary journey to Cyprus, Antioch in Pisidia, Lystra.
48	Famine in Judaea.
49	Claudius 'drives from Rome the Jewish agitators stirred up by Chrestos' (Suetonius).
49-50	The circumcision discussion between Paul and Barnabas, and Peter, James and John in Jerusalem. Called because of Luke's account the 'Council of Jerusalem'.
50	Dispute between Peter and Paul at Antioch.

50–52	Paul's second missionary journey to Lystra, Phrygia, Galatia, Macedonia and Athens.
	Finishes with eighteen months in Corinth. Paul writes the first letter to the Thessalonians.
52	Paul returns to Jerusalem and then goes to Antioch.
53–58	Paul's third missionary journey. Apollos at Ephesus and then at Corinth.
54–68	Nero is emperor.
54–57	Paul travels through Galatia and Phrygia visiting the churches. Then he stays at Ephesus for over two years. Writes Philippians and 1 Corinthians.
57	Troubles in Corinth. Paul pays the church a quick visit and returns to Ephesus.
	Writes letter to the Galatians.
57	Passes through Macedonia and writes 2 Corinthians and Romans.
58	Returns to Jerusalem, landing at Caesarea. He brings with him the collection he has made from the gentile churches.
	Paul is arrested in the Temple on the feast of Pentecost.
	He is brought before the Sanhedrin and also before Felix, the Roman governor.
	Deadlock ensues.
58–60	Paul a prisoner at Caesarea.
60	He appears before Festus, the new governor, and appeals to Caesar.
60	Paul sails for Rome as a privileged prisoner. Shipwreck at Malta, where he spends the winter.
61–63	Paul at Rome, under house arrest.
62	James the Just, the brother of the Lord, is stoned to death; eighty Pharisees appeal on his behalf to the Sanhedrin and die also.

64	Burning of Rome. Nero orders the persecution of the Christians.
	Possible death of Paul during the persecution of Nero.
66	Riots begin in Caesarea which start the great Jewish revolt.
68	Suicide of Nero. Two rival emperors, Otho and Vitellius, proclaimed.
69–79	Vespasian is emperor.
70	Destruction of Jerusalem. The inhabitants killed, sold as slaves or condemned to hard labour.
	The Gospel of St Mark written, probably in Rome.
79-81	Titus is emperor.
81-89	The Gospels of Matthew and Luke written.
89	Christians expelled from the synagogues.
100	The Gospel of St John written.

Select
bibliography

ALLEGRO, John, *The Dead Sea Scrolls*, Penguin, 1956.

BORNKAMM, Gunther, *Jesus of Nazareth*, (trans.) Hodder & Stoughton, 1960; *Paul*, (trans.) Hodder & Stoughton, 1971.

BULTMANN, R., *Theology of the New Testament*, (trans.) SCM Press, 1952.

CAIRD, G. B., *St Luke*, Pelican, 1963.

CARMICHAEL, Joel, *The Death of Jesus*, Victor Gollancz, 1963.

COHN, Haim, *The Trial and Death of Jesus*, Ktav Publishing House, New York, 1977.

DAVIES, W. D., *Paul and Rabbinic Judaism*, SPCK, 1948.

DAVIS, Charles, *The Body as Spirit*, Hodder & Stoughton, 1976.

FENTON, J. C., *St Matthew*, Pelican, 1968.

GRANT, Michael, *St Paul*, Weidenfeld & Nicolson, 1976; *Jesus*, Weidenfeld & Nicolson, 1977.

HENGEL, Martin, *The Son of God*, SCM Press, 1976.

HICK, John (ed.), *The Myth of God Incarnate*, SCM Press, 1977.

HOOKER, M. and WILSON, (eds), *Paul and Paulinism*, SPCK, 1982.

HORBURY, W. and McNEIL, B. (eds), *Suffering and Martyrdom in the New Testament*, Cambridge University Press, 1981.

JOSEPHUS, Flavius, *The Jewish War*, (trans.) Penguin, 1970.

KASEMANN, Ernst, *Perspectives on Paul*, (trans.) SCM Press, 1971.

KEMPIS, Thomas à, *The Imitation of Christ*, (trans.) Penguin, 1952.

KENNEDY, H. A. A., *St Paul and the Mystery Religions*, Hodder & Stoughton, 1913.

KNOX, Wilfred L., *St Paul and the Chruch of the Gentiles*, Cambridge University Press, 1939.

MACCOBY, Hyam, *Revolution in Judaea*, Ocean Books, 1973; *The Sacred Executioner*, Thames & Hudson, 1982.

MOORE, George Foot, *Judaism*, (3 vols) Oxford University Press, 1927–30.

MOULE, C. F. D., *The Origin of Christology*, Cambridge University Press, 1977.

NINEHAM, Dennis, *St Mark*, Pelican, 1963.

PAGELS, Elaine, *The Gnostic Gospels*, Weidenfeld & Nicolson, 1980.

ROBINSON, James M., *A New Quest for the Historical Jesus*, SCM Press, 1959.

SANDERS, E. P., *Paul and Palestinian Judaism*, SCM Press, 1977.

SCHWEITZER, A., *The Quest of the Historical Jesus*, (trans.) A. & C. Black, 1954; *The Mysticism of Paul the Apostle*, (trans.) A. & C. Black, 1956; *Paul and his Interpreters*, (trans.) A. & C. Black, 1967.

STANIFORTH, Maxwell (translator), *Early Christian Writings*, Penguin, 1968.

VERMES, G., *Jesus the Jew*, Collins, 1973.

WILSON, R. Mc. L., *Gnosis and the New Testament*, Blackwell, 1968.

WEISS, Johannes, *Jesus' Proclamation of the Kingdom of God*, (trans.) SCM Press, 1971.

Index